Sustaining Gains in Poverty Reduction and Human Development in the Middle East and North Africa

Sustaining Gains in Poverty Reduction and Human Development in the Middle East and North Africa

Farrukh Iqbal

THE WORLD BANK

Washington, D.C.

ISBN: 0-8213-6527-4
ISBN-13: 978-0-8213-6527-4
e-ISBN: 0-8213-6528-2
DOI: 10.1596/978-0-8213-6527-4

Library of Congress Cataloging-in-Publication data has been applied for.

Contents

List of Figures

List of Boxes

Preface

The Middle East and North Africa Regional Vice Presidency of the World Bank has published a number of studies in recent years that describe and analyze key aspects of the social and economic development experience of the region as a whole. This effort has so far covered studies of growth, employment, trade, governance, gender, pensions, HIV/AIDS, and social protection. This book is the latest output of this ongoing analytic enterprise. It focuses on the experience of the Middle East and North Africa with poverty and human development. It deals mostly with the period since the mid-1980s, a period that has seen significant changes in the region's economic, political, and demographic context.

The focus on poverty is a natural one for the World Bank. However, some may not think poverty a prominent enough issue in the Middle East and North Africa, given the region's association with oil wealth. This book shows that this image is a misleading one. Although the Middle East and North Africa has a low rate of poverty when compared with other developing regions, the fact remains that one of every five persons there can be considered poor (at the $2 PPP international poverty line) and that this situation has not improved much since the late 1980s. This may be thought of as the social cost of the low rates of economic growth that have prevailed in the region over this period and it justifies the abiding concern of the World Bank and many of the region's governments with promoting growth as a means to reducing poverty.

The book also draws attention to a paradox. While income poverty did not improve in the last decade, human development indicators for the region improved tremendously, at a rate that surpassed even that of lower middle income comparators. The analysis presented in the book suggests that, among other factors, improvements in the delivery of public health and education services are likely to have played a part in this remarkable achievement. This is an encouraging finding. It suggests that, even in the absence of income growth, the health and education aspects of the living standards of the poor can be enhanced through attention to service delivery. It is a finding that provides a strong empirical justification for the World Bank's operational focus on health, education and social safety net issues in the Middle East and North Africa Region.

So the twin challenges for the region in the future are that of obtaining higher growth while building on human development achievements. Now that growth rates have begun to pick up in the region, the prospects for poverty reduction in the future have improved as well. But we have to be mindful of the sustainability of the growth path. If growth in the region is based largely on favorable terms of trade shifts for hydrocarbons, the sustainability of such growth may be questioned. We saw a demonstration of this after 1985 when a terms-of-trade shift against hydrocarbons led to economic stagnation for the next fifteen years. But if growth comes from a broader economic base and is led by the private sector, it is more likely to be durable.

Sustaining gains in human development will require tackling new challenges. In education, the focus must now shift from quantity to quality. In health, attention must continue to be paid to the access needs of the poor and to the new diseases arising from changing demographics and shifts in diets and other lifestyle choices. In social protection, more emphasis must be placed on efficiency and insurance objectives than has hitherto been the case in the region.

But this is not all that needs to be done. Economic, political and social inequalities tend to trap disadvantaged people at the bottom of society for generation after generation. This is not only unfortunate for those at the bottom; it is also an impediment to higher economic growth over the long run. When those with ability are denied the opportunity to contribute fully to the economy, the economy suffers. Most Middle Eastern and North African countries have taken big strides toward equalizing opportunities through providing better health and education to their citizens. But meaningful opportunities do not flow from better education and health alone. They are affected as well by the scope for voice, inclusion, and accountability at all levels of decision making. This remains a challenge for the region—one that must be tackled more comprehensively in the future if we are to give full meaning to the term "human development."

Christiaan J. Poortman
Vice President
Middle East and North Africa Region

Acknowledgments

This book was written by Farrukh Iqbal on the basis of background papers and analytical inputs from Surjit Bhalla, Tazeen Fasih, Claudia Nassif, Gillian Perkins, Nagwa Riad, and Marie Rosencrantz. The book has benefited greatly from the advice and guidance of Mustapha Kamel Nabli, Chief Economist of the Middle East and North Africa Region of the World Bank, and from comments and suggestions provided at various review stages by Richard Adams, Asad Alam, Abdulrehman M. Almofadhi, Paloma Anos Casero, Pierre Audinet, Regina Bendokat, John Blomquist, Nadereh Chamlou, Dipak Dasgupta, Omer Karasappan, Jennie Litvack, Akiko Maeda, Stefano Paternostro, Setareh Razmara, Michal Rutkowski, Carlos Silva-Jauregui, Miho Tanaka, Michel Welmond, and Gianni Zanini. Valuable assistance was provided on data-related matters by Paul Dyer and G.V. Rao, and on document preparation by Angela Hawkins. The World Bank's Office of the Publisher managed editorial and print production, including book design.

Abbreviations and Acronyms

BAJ	Barnamaj Al Aoulaouiyat Ijtimaiya
DHS	Demographic and Health Survey
EEP	Education Enhancement Program
GDP	gross domestic product
LPG	liquefied petroleum gas
MENA	Middle East and North Africa
MENA7	Algeria, the Arab Republic of Egypt, the Islamic Republic of Iran, Jordan, Morocco, Tunisia, and the Republic of Yemen
MENA10	Algeria, the Arab Republic of Egypt, the Islamic Republic of Iran, Jordan, Lebanon, Libya, Morocco, Syria, Tunisia, and the Republic of Yemen
MFI	microfinance institution
MOSAI	Ministry of Social Affairs and Insurance
NAF	National Aid Fund
PHC	primary health care
PN	*Promotion Nationale*
PPP	purchasing power parity
PPP$	purchasing power parity dollars
SWF	Social Welfare Fund

Executive Summary

The main objective of this book is to review and learn from the Middle East and North Africa Region's experience with poverty reduction and human development. A capsule version of the modern economic history of this region would divide the past 40 years or so into two periods—a statist period that prevailed until the mid-1980s and a transition period from then to the present. The *statist period* was characterized, as the name suggests, by state domination of the economic system, an inward-looking economic strategy, and heavy reliance on plan-based public investments as the main engine of growth. The *transition period*, now approximately two decades old, has been marked in different countries by efforts of varying intensity and resolve to move toward more open and market-oriented economic regimes, with a corresponding enhancement in the role of the private sector. It is convenient to frame the region's experience with poverty reduction and human development in terms of these two periods as well.

The coverage of this book is limited by the availability of data. Some countries in the Middle East and North Africa do not collect systematic data on poverty, and have only rudimentary information on health and education inputs and outcomes. Many others collect adequate data but restrict public access to it. This report focuses on a subset of countries from the Middle East and North Africa Region for which relevant data on poverty and human development are available to the World Bank.

Poverty data in aggregate form are available in the World Bank for seven Middle Eastern and North African countries, namely, Algeria, the Arab Republic of Egypt, the Islamic Republic of Iran, Jordan, Morocco, Tunisia, and the Republic of Yemen. Adequate data related to spending and outcomes for human development are available for an additional three countries, namely, Lebanon, Libya, and the Syrian Arab Republic. Thus the term *MENA* is used in this report to refer to the set of 7 countries when poverty is being discussed and to the larger set of 10 countries when human development is being discussed. In neither case does the report cover Bahrain, Djibouti, Kuwait, Oman, Saudi Arabia, and the United Arab Emirates, nor, except briefly, Iraq and West Bank/Gaza. The 10 included countries account for approximately 85 percent of the total population of the region.

Available data show the following features of the statist period:

- *Rapid economic growth occurred.* Average per capita gross domestic product (GDP) for the region rose more than sevenfold, from $1.6 a day in 1965 (in constant 1993 purchasing power parity [PPP] dollars) to $11.7 a day by 1985. For much of this period, growth was driven by high rates of investment made possible for some countries by high prices for hydrocarbons and for other countries by high levels of borrowing.

- *Poverty declined.* Pre-1985 household surveys are only available for Tunisia and Egypt, and these clearly show declining poverty rates during 1965–85. In Tunisia, poverty fell from 51 percent in 1965 to only 16 percent in 1985. Egypt's achievement was also impressive, with poverty declining from 82 percent to 53 percent between 1975 and 1985. An aggregate picture of regional poverty shows a poverty incidence rate of only 25 percent for MENA by 1987, the lowest among all developing regions at that time.

- *Remarkable progress took place with respect to human development indicators.* Between 1965 and 1985, adult literacy almost doubled, going from 24 percent to 47 percent; average schooling completed by those over 15 years of age rose more than fourfold, from 0.8 to 3.4 years; mortality rates for children less than 5 years old fell from 233 per thousand live births to 108; and life expectancy rose from approximately 50 years to 61 years. In comparative terms, the region easily kept pace with the performance of middle-income countries in East Asia and Latin America.

- *The archetypal social policy model of the region came into full effect.* This model comprised three main components: an education and health component in which free education and primary health care services were promised to all citizens; a consumption-subsidy component in which key consumption items, such as food and energy, were provided at subsidized rates to most citizens; and a public employment component through which permanent jobs (and associated old-age pension benefits) were provided to many citizens.

The transition period featured not only meager growth in per capita GDP and little change in poverty but also, remarkably, continued rapid improvements in human development. Attempts to transition from the statist to a market-oriented economic regime gathered momentum in the mid-1980s as growth collapsed following a decline in the price of hydro-carbons—a key resource for many countries in the region—and debt burdens became unsustainable in a context of low productivity growth. Over the next 15 years or so, the following features were evident:

- *Per capita output stagnated.* By 2000, the region's average per capita output had only reached $11.3 per day (PPP$) and had not fully recovered to its 1985 level. The slow growth was due in part to low prices for hydrocarbons, in part to declining remittances and aid flows, and in part to the limited extent of structural reforms undertaken in the region as well as a low payoff to the reforms that were implemented.

- *Very little progress was made on the poverty front.* The region's average poverty rate fluctuated between 20 and 25 percent during the entire decade of the 1990s. By 2001, approximately 52 million people were poor, an increase in absolute numbers of approximately 11.5 million people, compared with the situation in 1987.

- *The Gini measure of inequality fluctuated between 0.32 and 0.44 for most MENA countries*, although it was lower in the 1990s than in the 1970s for the three countries (Egypt, Iran, and Tunisia) for which an adequate time series is available. On the whole, the lack of any systematic deterioration in inequality after 1985 suggests that structural reforms adopted in this period did not have an adverse impact on inequality.

- *Human development indicators continued to improve.* Between 1985 and 2000, literacy spread to 69 percent of the population, average years of schooling (for those above age 15) rose to 5.2, child mortality rates plunged to approximately 46 deaths per thousand children in the first five years of life, and life expectancy climbed to 68 years. Remarkably, the region improved its human indicators faster than did middle-income comparators over this period, and it did so despite a considerably slower rate of output growth and a decline in levels of public spending.

- *The region's social safety nets came under stress as fiscal resources tightened.* In response to fiscal tightening, safety nets were modified in several countries to reduce budget outlays on certain subsidies, tighten eligibility for others, replace in-kind subsidies with cash transfers, reduce public sector employment, and provide temporary jobs through public works programs and longer-term help through microfinance schemes.

The fact that little growth or poverty reduction was achieved during the 1990s despite impressive gains in human development suggests that the region had difficulties in translating rising human capital into higher productivity. This is supported by two pieces of evidence: the region exhibits low rates of return on education (ranging from 2.5 to 10.0 percent for different levels of schooling); and it has experienced high rates of unemployment (currently just above 13 percent), especially among educated people. Low growth, occasioned in part by macroeconomic policy and structural factors, is an important determinant of both unemployment and low rates of return on education. Among structural factors, recent academic research suggests that the impact of education on income is strongly conditioned by an economy's degree of openness. Insufficient openness to trade and investment has likely constrained returns on education in the Middle East and North Africa Region.

There is reason to believe that the strong gains in education and health since the mid-1980s were due in part to greater efficiency in the delivery of such services. There is a more encouraging aspect as well to the MENA experience with human development in the transition period. Econometric analysis conducted for this report shows that most MENA countries had gains higher than can be explained by initial incomes, initial levels of education and health, income growth during 1980–2000, and average public spending on education (used as a proxy for spending on social services). In part, such gains may have come from a better targeting of spending to deliver services to underserved groups. In part also, such gains may have resulted from positive cross-sector externalities. For example, statistical analysis shows a strong link between child mortality improvements during 1980–2000 and the level of female education achieved by 1980. In other words, investments in female education during the pre-1980 period had an important impact on health gains in the period thereafter.

Opportunities to make social safety nets more efficient instruments for poverty reduction and human development have largely been missed. The parts of the region's safety nets that are effective are not efficient, and the parts that are relatively efficient are not effective. For example, food and energy subsidies reach a large number of people and are effective in the sense that they also reach the poor. However, both food and energy subsidies are inefficient in that they involve a lot of resource leakage to the nonpoor populace. The benefit transfers from energy subsidies, in particular, are heavily tilted toward the nonpoor: as much as 93 percent of gasoline subsidies in Egypt go to the richest quintile of consumers. At the same time, although cash transfers are relatively better targeted to the poor and the vulnerable, they are funded at such low levels (often less than 1 percent of GDP) that they are not very effective in improving the conditions of the poor. And whereas some improvements in efficiency have taken place in the past with respect to the design of food subsidies, especially in Egypt and Tunisia, opportunities to make a substantial difference through reforming energy subsidies, involving a much greater fiscal payoff, have largely been missed.

Accelerating the pace of poverty reduction in the future requires an acceleration of growth. The strategy for higher growth in the region comprises three key elements, namely, an enlargement of the role of the private sector, a shift from import-substitution strategies to greater global integration, and a move away from excessive reliance on hydrocarbons to a more diversified base of economic activities. Most countries in the region are already embarked on these three realignments, but more vigorous steps need to be taken in the future to complete the desired transitions. In recent reports the World Bank has calculated that an acceleration of the three realignments noted above, combined with better governance and efforts to increase female labor force participation, could increase the annual average output per capita by 3 percent or three times the actual rate experienced since 1985. Such a difference in growth can make a tremendous difference in poverty outcomes within a decade or so. For example, such a difference in growth rates can mean a difference of 8 percentage points in poverty for the region as a whole by 2015. Translated into numbers, this means that the higher growth rate will help lift an additional 22 million people out of poverty. A higher growth rate also will enable the countries in the region to tackle the more resource-intensive challenge of providing good health care and education in the future.

Growth policies also must be accompanied by policies to increase labor absorption in the private sector. In the short run, the new growth paradigm may be associated with greater volatility in jobs and incomes. Such churning is healthy and helps reallocate capital, labor, and entrepreneurial talent in accordance with changes in comparative advantage brought about by changes in the global economic environment and by domestic policy reforms. But it also could generate adverse short-run changes in employment and incomes among the poor and the near-poor (that is, those living just above the poverty line). For example, trade liberalization may cause some people to lose jobs in sectors that were previously protected, even though the liberalizing measure might be poverty reducing and welfare improving for poor people as a whole. The impact of transitional job losses can be mitigated by measures to increase the private sector's demand for labor in general, and measures to improve the employability of workers through more flexible labor market laws and procedures in particular. Although more flexibility has been introduced in some countries in recent years, rigidities with respect to dismissals and layoffs continue to affect the levels and types of employment offered by the private sector. Many countries continue to ban dismissal for business reasons or make it administratively difficult and expensive. As a result, formal private sector employment is lower than it needs to be; and informal sector employment, with its attendant vulnerabilities, is higher than necessary. Similar but gender-based rigidities have prevented female labor force participation from rising to levels more compatible with the impressive gains made in female education in the region.

Sustaining gains in human development will require paying attention to new challenges. The good historical performance of the region may not necessarily ensure similar performance in the future. The education and health challenges of the future are likely to be different from those in the past, and they will require different responses. In particular, these responses must factor in the effects of the ongoing demographic transition, the need to compete globally, and the need to become more efficient in the use of available resources.

Sustaining gains in education requires shifting the focus from quantity to quality. As noted earlier, most countries in the region have a strong record of improving the quantity of education provided. The challenge of the future, however, will be more in the area of education quality and labor market relevance. As Middle Eastern and North African economies move toward producing more goods and services for world markets, they will need to compete with other countries to secure market share and obtain larger flows of foreign investment. The higher the level of skills in their workforces, the better placed these countries will be to compete internationally. Improving the quality of education in public schools is important for poverty reduction and equity as well. Low quality in public schools is a special problem for poor children because they rarely have alternative higher-quality options in the form of private schools or private tutoring. Moreover, receiving a low-quality education at the primary and secondary levels effectively prevents children from poor backgrounds from passing the competitive examinations typically required for entrance to tertiary institutions.

Sustaining gains in health requires continued attention to the needs of the poor and the consequences of the ongoing demographic transition. Although the region has performed well in improving the access of the average citizen to primary care facilities and public health interventions, more needs to be done in the future on two fronts: further improving access for the poor, and coping with an emerging disease pattern that is linked to lifestyle choices and an aging population. Despite progress in the past four decades, significant disparities continue to exist between rich and poor people with regard to health outcomes such as child mortality and malnutrition. For the most part, removing these disparities will require adequate funding of public health budgets, a continued special focus on maternal and child health services, and specific efforts to target regions and neighborhoods with a preponderance of poor residents (such as most rural areas and urban slums). In addition to direct health interventions, it will be important to continue addressing issues such as the supply of safe water and sanitation to underserved groups and to provide nutrition and preventive health education.

Coping with the disease patterns arising from the region's ongoing demographic and epidemiologic transition, however, will require the development of new approaches to health care financing. Because treatment of the emerging noncommunicable disease patterns is likely to be individual oriented and technology intensive, it will be more costly. Accordingly, there will be more pressure on budgetary resources, pressure that may take away funds that presently address the public health needs of the poor. Among ways to relieve such pressure is to develop insurance mechanisms to spread the financial cost of treatment across a diversified pool of users and establish charges for the use of university or highly specialized hospital services for those who can afford to pay. Because the new disease patterns also are spreading among the poor populations, it will be important to develop a system that provides them with low-cost access to treatment services. Also relevant would be the redesign of existing subsidies (for example, on pharmaceuticals in Iran) so as to minimize leakage to those who are not poor.

Social safety nets should be made more important instruments of the poverty-reduction strategy in the future through a focus on efficiency and insurance objectives. Although measures directed at increasing growth and enhancing the access of the poor to health care and education will remain the two principal pillars of the region's poverty-reduction strategy, attention also must be paid to the third pillar, namely, social safety nets. These have to be reformed with two objectives in mind: increasing the efficiency with which limited resources are directed to the needs of poor and vulnerable people, and improving their ability to cope with adverse income shocks that may occur as regional economies become more private sector, trade, and market oriented. Improved efficiency would imply a greater impact on poverty reduction for any given level of economic growth and volume of fiscal resources devoted to the task. It also could release resources to help those who need safety net assistance and to increase pro-poor spending in other areas, such as public health, improved water supply, and better rural infrastructure.

Safety nets can be made more efficient through better targeting, but this is presently constrained by political economy considerations and by deficiencies in data access and quality and related technical and administrative concerns. Politically, the adoption of pro-poor targeting as a policy objective may provoke discontent and resistance among better-off, more vocal, and politically stronger groups who might stand to lose from such a move. Factors like that have come into play in the region in the past—during attempts to reform food subsidies, for example. In some cases they led to the abandonment of targeting, but in others they led to more sophisticated program design and flexibility in implementation.

The technical and administrative dimensions relate to the design and cost of targeting mechanisms as well as to the availability and use of appropriate data. Although narrower targeting can improve the efficiency of subsidy programs, this has to be balanced against the cost of implementing appropriate targeting schemes. In countries with weak administrative and governance structures, this may be a big challenge. Efficient targeting also requires good data to identify and locate the poor, good analysis to calibrate the connection between policy and poverty outcomes, and organizational arrangements to learn from experience and modify policies as needed. The Middle East and North Africa presently suffer from deficiencies in all these areas. Data that would allow distinguishing between the chronically poor and the temporarily poor are not collected anywhere in the region except the Islamic Republic of Iran. And the household data that are collected are typically not made public, thereby preventing the breadth and depth of analysis that can substantially strengthen the knowledge base for antipoverty policy formulation. By and large, in most Middle Eastern and North African countries, access to data is not considered a matter of public right but of bureaucratic discretion.

Finally, the effectiveness of antipoverty programs is often hampered by the lack of internal systems to collect and analyze relevant data and to link program design to lessons of experience. In many Middle Eastern and North African countries, the issue is not so much the lack of programs to help the poor as it is the lack of information about whether existing efforts are helping the poor in a cost-effective manner. This can best be remedied through an effort to foster more of an "evaluation culture" within government agencies. Such a culture could be encouraged, for example, by making rigorous baseline surveys and periodic evaluations mandatory in all publicly funded antipoverty programs.

Safety nets also can be strengthened through measures that help ensure against the risks of job and income loss. For example, unemployment insurance schemes, paid for by contributions from firms and workers, can help cushion the transition from one job to another. To date, there is not much experience with such schemes in the region, and care will have to be exercised to keep programs consistent with financial sustainability, equity, and incentives for workers to move out of unemployment. Temporary employment programs also can help. There is much more experience with these programs in the region, and this experience can be used to make the programs both more effective, through a focus on the labor intensity of projects, and more efficient, through an emphasis on targeting to the poor through appropriate wage setting.

Last, the ability to cope with unanticipated shocks is often eased by access to finance. In the case of entrepreneurs from among the poor and near-poor, the relevant resource is microfinance because, without collateral, they rarely have access to loans from commercial banks. In recent years the scale and reach of microfinance schemes have been growing in the Middle East and North Africa. Most governments there have progressively reduced policy impediments to the growth of microfinance institutions, and approximately 19 percent of the potential client base is now being served, up from 3 percent only a decade or so ago.

This survey of poverty and human development trends in the Middle East and North Africa suggests reasons for both concern and optimism. The concern arises from the fact that the growth performance of the region was weak during the last two decades and this exacted a social cost in terms of lack of progress in poverty reduction. Almost 11.5 million people were added to the ranks of the poor between 1987 and 2001 because the region's population continued to grow while its economies did not. Optimism arises from the facts that, despite stagnant growth, human development in the region continued to progress at an impressive pace and that some of this was likely due to gains in the efficiency with which health and education services are delivered. If the region builds on these human development achievements and implements macroeconomic and structural reform measures to climb to a higher growth trajectory, it could well become the first developing region to make poverty history.

CHAPTER 1

Income Poverty Trends and Patterns

Data Availability

Direct estimates of poverty can only be derived from nationally representative household income and expenditure surveys. For the Middle East and North Africa Region, the earliest such surveys recorded in the World Bank's Global Poverty Monitoring Database are for the mid-to-late 1980s for five countries: Morocco, 1984–85; Tunisia, 1985; the Islamic Republic of Iran, 1986; Jordan, 1986–87; and Algeria, 1988 (see table 1.1). The Arab Republic of Egypt first enters the database in 1990–91.[1] As we move into the decade of the 1990s, the data situation improves considerably as several household surveys were conducted in Algeria, Egypt, the Islamic Republic of Iran, Jordan, Morocco, and Tunisia. For the Republic of Yemen, two surveys are available, for 1992 and 1998, but the first one is considered unreliable because of an unrepresentative sampling frame.[2] These seven countries provide the core data that have been used for the analysis of regional poverty trends and characteristics in this book. At the time of this writing, sufficient information was not available from other Middle Eastern and North African countries to be able to include them in the regional analysis. A general discussion of issues related to the availability and accessibility of household data in the region is provided in box 1.1. For three cases—Iraq, the Syrian Arab Republic, and West Bank/Gaza, some poverty information is provided in box 1.2.

Snapshot of Poverty in the 1980s

Poverty head count ratios at the conventional $1/day line (technically $1.08 in 1993 constant purchasing power parity [PPP] dollars per person per day) are shown in table 1.2 for six countries—Algeria, Egypt, the Islamic Republic of Iran, Jordan, Morocco, and Tunisia—for the period

TABLE 1.1

Household Survey Years by Middle Eastern and North African Country

Country	Survey Years
Algeria	1988, 1995, 2000
Arab Republic of Egypt	1990–91, 1995–96, 1999–2000
Islamic Republic of Iran	1986, 1990, 1994, 1998
Jordan	1986–87, 1992, 1997, 2002
Morocco	1984–85, 1990–91, 1998–99, 2000–01
Tunisia	1985, 1990, 1995, 2000
Republic of Yemen	1992, 1998

Source: World Bank.

1990–91 and before. *The data clearly reveal that these six countries had achieved very low levels of absolute poverty by the mid- to late 1980s.*

The dramatically low poverty estimates for the Middle East and North Africa raise the question of whether the $1 poverty line is a meaningful

BOX 1.1

Availability of Poverty Data in the Middle East and North Africa Region

The design of antipoverty programs is strongly affected by the availability of data on poverty. The foundation of good policies is good analysis, and such analysis can be facilitated by making relevant data publicly available. The greater the numbers of researchers who have access to such data, the greater the probability that the data will be subjected to a broad variety of analytic techniques and consistency checks and, therefore, will yield more robust results. Where access to data is constrained, the ability to analyze and use data atrophies because there is little or no pressure from competitive research to improve analytic skills and techniques. Local and international researchers migrate to topics where data are more easily available, thus depriving the country of possible improvements in the understanding of poverty reduction.

In the Middle East and North Africa Region, access to poverty data is severely limited. Different countries in the region fall into one or the other of three categories with respect to data access protocols. In some countries, poverty data are collected infrequently or not at all. In other countries, data are collected but are retained within government agencies and are not made public. In still others, data are collected but shared only in a limited fashion and with a restricted group, such as international development agencies. To the best of our knowledge, in no Middle Eastern or North African country does the public have unfettered access to household survey-based poverty data.

The Middle East and North Africa fares poorly in comparison to other regions even in sharing poverty data with international agencies. The table below shows the number of countries in each of six global regions that provide to the World Bank comprehensive access measure of the scope of the poverty challenge in the region. To provide a perspective on this, we report poverty head count rates at the $2/day line (technically $2.16 in 1993 constant PPP dollars per person per day), first for specific countries (see table 1.3) and then for the Middle East and North Africa as a whole in comparison with other developing regions (see figure 1.1).

Two points may be made on the basis of the poverty estimates derived from the $2 poverty line. First, country-specific poverty rates are now seen to be more of a challenge. This is especially true for Egypt where an additional 38 percent of the population is now measured as being poor. Indeed, the jump in poverty rates between the $1 and $2 lines suggests a high degree of vulnerability in the cases of most of the countries shown in table 1.3. Second, the region had the lowest poverty rates among all developing regions as it closed out the decade of the 1980s.[3]

to national household survey microdata for at least one survey year (out of the total number of countries in the region that conduct household surveys). As can be seen, the Middle East and North Africa Region is the most restrictive in providing access.

Region	Number of Countries (percentage)
East Asia and Pacific	5 of 10 (50)
Europe and Central Asia	22 of 25 (88)
Latin America and the Caribbean	21 of 23 (91)
Middle East and North Africa	3 of 8 (38)
South Asia	4 of 7 (57)
Sub-Saharan Africa	18 of 31 (58)

The World Bank database covers most countries in the Middle East and North Africa but typically only to the extent of having aggregate data on means and distributions of household incomes and/or expenditures with which to calculate poverty incidence rates at "international" PPP$ poverty lines. Unit records containing information on other individual and household characteristics often are not available. Although several Middle Eastern and North African countries cooperate with international development agencies in allowing access to unit record data for official work, such access tends to be on a case-by-case basis requring the approval of national authorities. This limits the flexibility and speed with which analysis can be conducted, and as a result, these countries often are missing from globally comparative work on the trends, structure, and causes of poverty. Lack of access to microdata also has an adverse effect on the quality of the analysis that can be performed because it renders the analyst unable to control for the potentially wide range of individual and household characteristics that are correlated with policy or program placement as well as with outcomes of interest.

BOX 1.2

Poverty in Iraq, Syria, and West Bank/Gaza

Iraq. Any discussion of poverty in Iraq must contend with the security situation that has prevailed in the country over the past few years. It is hard to collect truly representative data on poverty when some parts of the country are difficult to visit and when there is substantial ongoing movement of internally displaced people, refugees, and returnees. The best available evidence suggests that Iraq has an incidence of absolute poverty that is between 8 and 10 percent, and an additional 12–15 percent of the population appears to be close enough to the $1 poverty line to be considered vulnerable (World Bank 2005). This puts Iraq at the high end of the range for countries in the Middle East and North Africa. Two notable features of the poverty profile in Iraq are a distinct regional pattern, with the northern Kurdish areas being relatively better off and the southern governorates having much higher poverty incidence rates; and a distinct gender pattern, with female-headed households having median incomes that are 15 –25 percent below comparable male-headed households.

Syria. A recent study sponsored by the United Nations Development Programme (El-Laithy and Abu-Ismail 2005) provided poverty data for Syria for 2003–04. The study found a poverty rate of 11.4 percent at a national poverty line that covers basic food and nonfood needs. Many people are found to be clustered just below the poverty line, thus rendering the poverty estimate volatile and liable to change sharply in the event of an economic shock. Also reported were sharp regional differences in poverty incidence, with the northeastern region being most poor and the urban part of the southern region being least poor. Poverty is also highest among the illiterate and very low among university graduates. Finally, a gender aspect is noticeable: widows, as heads of households, with children, were reported to be very likely to be poor.

West Bank/Gaza. Although the security situation in the West Bank and Gaza bears similarities to that in Iraq, the understanding of poverty is much better because of the existence of a recent and representative survey of household incomes and expenditures (conducted in December 2003). According to this study, approximately 47 percent of the population may be considered poor in terms of the official, local currency poverty line (World Bank 2004g). The level of vulnerability to poverty is also very high as many families live just above the poverty line. Characteristics associated strongly with poverty include large family size, low education, and unemployment, but not refugee or female-headed household status. Whereas a statistically rigorous time trend in poverty cannot be established on the basis of existing surveys, the sharp drop of about 33 percent in average real per capita income between 1999 and 2003 is likely to have resulted in an upward surge in poverty as well.

TABLE 1.2

Poverty Head Count Ratios at $1/Day Line, 1984–91

Country	1984–85	1985–86	1986–87	1988–89	1990–91
Algeria	—	—	—	1.8	—
Arab Republic of Egypt	—	—	—	—	4.0
Islamic Republic of Iran	—	—	1.5	—	1.6
Jordan	—	—	0	—	—
Morocco	2.0	—	—	—	0.1
Tunisia	—	1.7	—	—	1.3

Source: World Bank Global Poverty Monitoring Database.

Note: — Not available.

TABLE 1.3

Poverty Head Count Ratios at $2/Day Line, 1984–91

Country	1984–85	1985–86	1986–87	1988–89	1990–91
Algeria	—	—	—	13.9	—
Arab Republic of Egypt	—	—	—	—	42.6
Islamic Republic of Iran	—	—	12.4	—	11.7
Jordan	—	—	0.4	—	—
Morocco	16.5	—	—	—	7.5
Tunisia	—	16.1	—	—	11.6

Source: World Bank Global Poverty Monitoring Database.

Note: — Not available.

FIGURE 1.1

Comparisons of Poverty Rates among Developing Regions at $2/Day Line, 1990–91

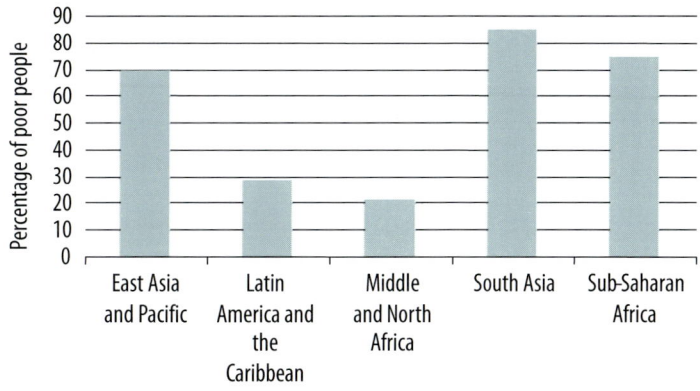

Source: World Bank Global Poverty Monitoring Database.

Poverty Trends

As noted earlier, direct estimates of poverty for this region are mostly available from the mid-1980s onward. For the period before the 1980s, comparable estimates of poverty based on per capita consumption expenditure are only possible for Tunisia (in 1965) and Egypt (in 1975). According to these data, the poverty rate was as high as 51.3 percent in Tunisia in 1965 and 82.2 percent in Egypt in 1975 (at the $2 line). Comparing these numbers to those achieved by the mid-1980s shows that considerable poverty reduction occurred during the early period.

What was the trend after the mid-1980s? Figure 1.2 shows that average poverty rates for the Middle East and North Africa have fluctuated since 1987: they decreased for about six years and then they increased in the mid-1990s before declining again toward the turn of the decade.[4] Although poverty rates were slightly lower on average in 2001 than in 1987 (regardless of whether they are measured at the $1 or $2 level), the general picture is one of stagnation. *After having reached the lowest levels of absolute poverty among developing regions by the late 1980s, the region failed to make further progress in the period thereafter.*

Country-specific trends for six Middle Eastern and North African countries (not including the Republic of Yemen for which only one reliable estimate is available) are shown in figure 1.3 and reflect two main features: (a) There is a big difference between the poverty rate of Egypt and that of the other five countries; and (b) whereas individual country experiences differed after 1987, the poverty rates attained by 2001 all clustered between 5 percent and 18 percent for all countries except Egypt.[5]

It is also of interest to see whether the region performed better or worse in poverty reduction than did other developing regions. The patterns shown in figure 1.4 suggest that the Middle East and North Africa performed worse than most. Whereas East Asia and South Asia showed clear gains over the 1990s, and Latin America showed modest gains, the Middle East and North Africa stagnation was similar to that of Sub-Saharan Africa.

Trends in Inequality

A three-decades–long time series of Gini coefficients based on per capita consumption distributions is available for three countries, the Islamic Republic of Iran, Tunisia, and Egypt. In the Islamic Republic of Iran the Gini rose from 0.44 to 0.47 between 1970 and 1985 and then declined to 0.44 by 1998. In Tunisia the Gini rose from 0.42 to 0.44 between 1965

FIGURE 1.2

Regional Poverty Trends, 1987–2001

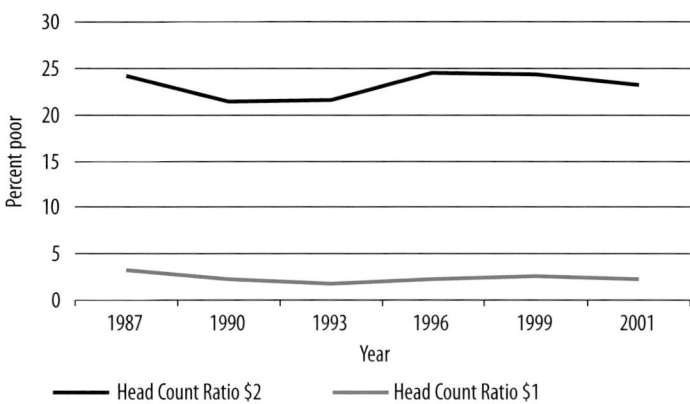

Source: World Bank Global Poverty Monitoring Database.

FIGURE 1.3

Country-Specific Poverty Trends at $2/Day Line, 1987–2001

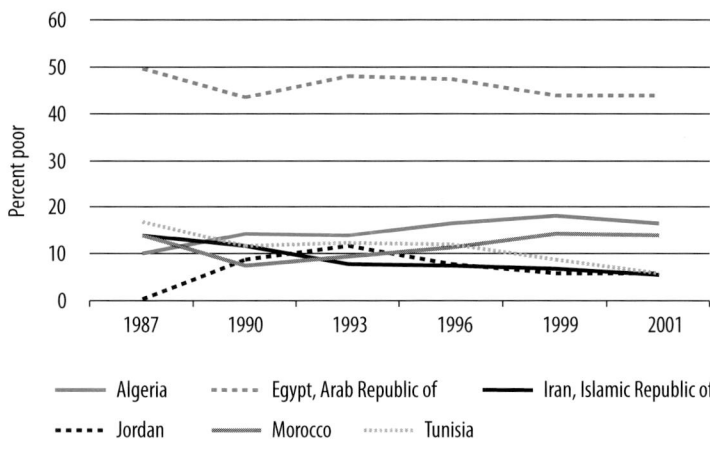

Source: World Bank Global Poverty Monitoring Database.

and 1975 but then gradually declined to around 0.41 by 2000. Egypt showed an improving trend between 1975 and 1985 followed by some worsening. In Morocco, the distribution of consumption has been stable since 1985, and in Algeria and Jordan there are not enough observations to establish a trend.

Three comments may be made on the basis of the pattern shown in figure 1.5. First, the level of inequality was higher in the 1970s than in the 1990s. Second, the structural reforms of the 1990s do not appear to be as-

FIGURE 1.4

Comparative Trends in Regional Poverty at $2/Day Line, 1987–2001

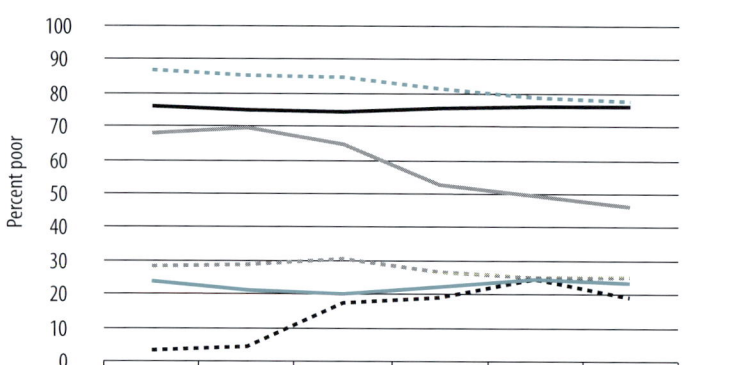

Source: World Bank Global Poverty Monitoring Database.

sociated with any systematic deterioration in inequality. Third, the region's range of inequality measures, currently between 0.34 and 0.44, put it in the middle segment of the global range of consumption Gini coefficients—better than most countries in Latin America and Sub-Saharan Africa but worse than most countries in South and East Asia.

FIGURE 1.5

Trends in Inequality, 1965–2000

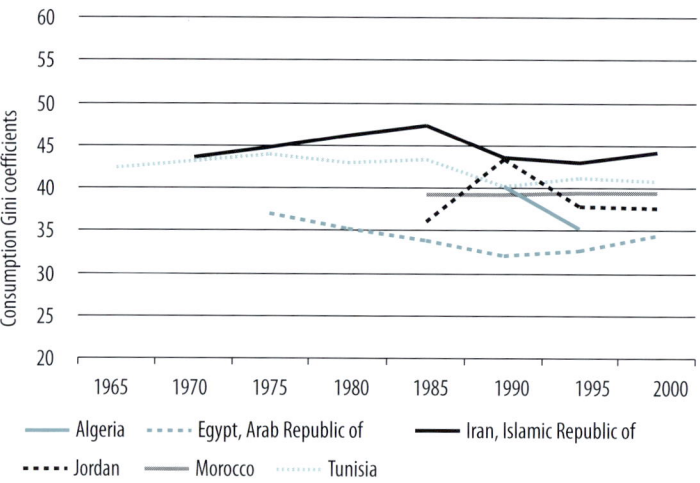

Source: World Bank Global Poverty Monitoring Database.

Poverty Levels from National Poverty Lines

The preceding discussion has been framed in terms of "international" poverty lines expressed in PPP$ terms. Although the resulting estimates are useful for cross-country comparisons, they are not necessarily as suitable for the framing of domestic policy discussions as are estimates founded on "national" poverty lines generated on the basis of locally relevant standards of food and nonfood consumption requirements. Such national poverty estimates are shown in the third column of table 1.4 for years in which survey data were available and analyzed in World Bank reports or other research investigations for the seven countries in the World Bank's database (with results for Iraq, Syria, and West Bank/Gaza, not in the Bank's database, reported in box 1.2). The results show national poverty levels that are similar (in the latest survey years) to those derived from the $2 PPP line for Algeria, Tunisia, and the Republic of Yemen, and are higher than the $2 line for the Islamic Republic of Iran, Jordan, and Morocco. For Egypt the relevant correspondence occurs between the $1 and $2 lines. *On the whole, centering poverty estimates on the $2 PPP line or higher provides a closer approximation to levels derived from national poverty lines than doing so on the $1 PPP line.*

Factors Underlying Poverty Trends in the Middle East and North Africa

The foregoing has shown that poverty rates in the Middle East and North Africa were reduced prior to 1985 but then stagnated within a 20–25 percent band measured at the $2 line. What explains this pattern? Arithmetically, changes in poverty may be attributed to changes in average incomes (growth) and changes in inequality (distribution). The available information shows that the region experienced extremely rapid growth in the pre-1985 period (see figure 1.6) and that inequality likely declined. So both growth and distributional effects pulled in the same, poverty-reducing, direction prior to 1985. But it was most likely the substantial improvement in growth that had the bigger impact on poverty in this period.

Growth slowed dramatically after 1985. Indeed, in constant PPP$ terms, per capita output had not recovered to the 1985 level even by the year 2000. This must have exercised a strong constraining effect on the increase in the consumption for the poor as well. If anything, inequality improved slightly over this period, exercising a modest pro-poor effect.

We can explore the determinants of poverty patterns further by looking at some factors related to growth and distribution. For example,

TABLE 1.4

Comparison of Poverty Estimates Using International and National Poverty Lines

(Percent)

Country and Year	Poverty Head Count at $1 per day	Poverty Head Count at $2 per day	Poverty Head Count at National Poverty Line
Algeria			
1988	2	14	8
1995	1	15	14
2000	—	—	12
Arab Republic of Egypt			
1990/91	4	43	25
1995/96	4	50	23
1999/2000	3	44	17
Islamic Republic of Iran			
1986	2	12	27
1990	2	12	26
1994	1	8	21
1998	0	7	21
Jordan			
1987	0	1	3
1992	1	11	14
1997	0	7	21
2002	1	7	14
Morocco			
1984/85	2	17	26
1990/91	0	8	13
1998/99	1	14	19
2000/01	—	—	18
Tunisia			
1985	2	16	11
1990	1	12	7
1995	1	13	8
2000	0	7	4
Republic of Yemen			
1998	10	45	42

Sources: International poverty line estimates from World Bank Global Poverty Monitoring Database. National poverty line estimates sourced as follows: Algeria: World Bank 2004a; Jordan: data for 1997 and 2002 from World Bank 2004d; Morocco: 2000/01 data from Royaume du Maroc 2005; Tunisia: World Bank 2003b. Remaining entries: Adams and Page 2003; Table 5.

Adams and Page (2003) have argued that the relatively low level of poverty in the Middle East and North Africa achieved by the mid-1980s was also the result of two region-specific characteristics, namely, high levels of public sector employment and high levels of remittances. Using a cross-country data set covering 50 developing countries for the year 1990, they reported a statistically significant negative relationship between government employment (as a share of total employment) and the poverty rate (measured at the $1 line) while controlling for per capita gross domestic product (GDP) and inequality (measured by Gini coefficient). They also reported a statistically significant shift factor for the region,

FIGURE 1.6

Regional Trends in GDP per Capita, 1965–2000
(PPP$)

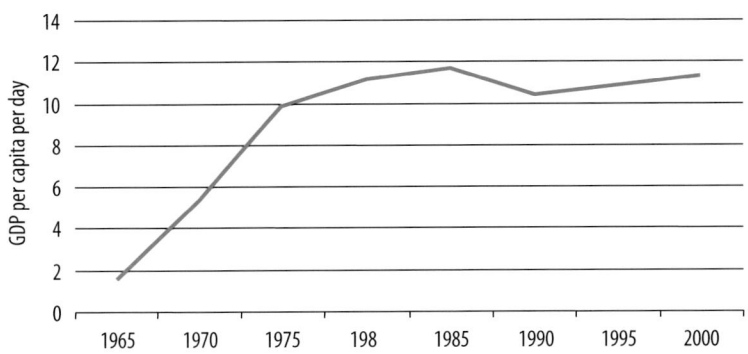

Source: Staff calculations.

Note: Weighted average for 10 MENA countries: Algeria, the Arab Republic of Egypt, the Islamic Republic of Iran, Jordan, Lebanon, Libya, Morocco, Syria, Tunisia, and the Republic of Yemen.

suggesting that the link between government employment and poverty is stronger in Middle Eastern and North African countries than in the sample as a whole. This finding supports their assertion that "since the early 1970s, a number of MENA countries...have used public sector employment (including government work) as a kind of blunt policy instrument for providing welfare employment to an ever-increasing proportion of the labor force" (Adams and Page 2003, pp. 2031).

A similar link is reported in the case of remittances, suggesting that private transfers via remittances have been an important source of poverty reduction in the region. Again the finding is consistent with what is known about the sources of growth in Middle East and North Africa in the period prior to 1985. The region experienced an economic boom between 1975 and 1985 on the basis of high oil prices. This boom spread throughout the region as workers from countries with large labor forces and/or low oil resources (such as Egypt and Jordan) flocked to work in the oil-producing countries of the Persian Gulf. At the same time, waves of poor workers from the Maghreb countries began migrating to Western Europe in search of jobs. Thus, large volumes of remittances were generated during 1975–90 and these are most likely to have accrued to relatively poor families in the labor-exporting countries.

To what extent do these factors explain trends observed in the subsequent period? At one level these findings are consistent with growth and poverty trends observed in the 1990s. During this period both public sector employment and remittances declined on average in the Middle East and North Africa Region, and may have contributed to the relative stagnation of income growth. For example, public sector employment declined in the 1990s in four of five Middle Eastern and North African countries for which suitable data are available, namely, Algeria, Jordan, Morocco, and Tunisia (World Bank 2004h, figure 4.6). Only in Egypt was there an increase in the public sector's share of total employment—an increase that is all the more surprising because Egypt was simultaneously involved in a structural adjustment program that featured a large fiscal contraction. Similarly, there was a decline in the ratio of workers' remittances to GDP in all the main remittance-receiving countries during the 1990s, with the exception of Jordan (see figure 1.7). In Egypt remittances declined from around 15 percent of GDP in 1992 to less than 5 percent by 2003. In the Republic of Yemen, remittances collapsed from around 31 percent of GDP in 1990 to only 12 percent by 2003.

However, the role of public sector employment in reducing poverty is ambiguous. In the short run, public employment may provide some of the poor with employment and steady income. Over the longer run, however, high public sector employment may actually raise poverty by lowering economic efficiency and thereby depressing growth. Reducing the role of the public sector in the economies of the Middle Eastern and North African countries was indeed an important part of the rationale for the structural adjustment programs undertaken in the region since the 1980s, programs aimed at generating new sources of growth for these countries. Herein lies a policy dilemma for the region: how best to balance the short-term advantages of using public employment as an instrument of social protection with the adverse longer-term impact on growth.

FIGURE 1.7

Worker Remittances as a Share of GDP, 1990–2003
(Percent)

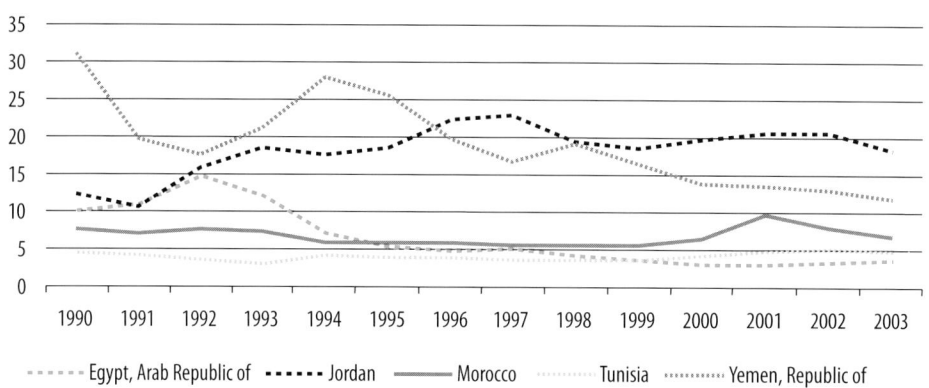

Source: International Monetary Fund.

Economic Vulnerability

It has been noted earlier that the definition of absolute poverty that is common in international comparisons, namely, the head count ratio at $1 PPP per capita per day, produces a very low estimate of poverty for most countries in the Middle East and North Africa. Indeed, these estimates are so low that they are likely to be misleading indicators of true economic deprivation in the region. When a $2 line is used, the proportion of people found to be poor rises significantly in most countries and very sharply in some (for example, Egypt and the Republic of Yemen). This suggests that measured poverty is very sensitive to the choice of the poverty line, at least at the $1 level.

Figure 1.8 provides a perspective on the sensitivity of poverty estimates to alternative poverty lines ranging from $1 to $4 and using the latest available household survey in the seven Middle Eastern and North African countries for which we have data. For Egypt and the Republic of Yemen it is clear that this sensitivity is greatest (slope is steepest) between $1 and $2, less but still substantial between $2 and $3, and least between $3 and $4. It also is clear that the sensitivity is greatest for Egypt and the Republic of Yemen between $1 and $3, but becomes similar among all countries beyond $3. Perhaps a more surprising result is that the sensitivity to choice of poverty lines for countries other than Egypt and the Republic of Yemen is higher between $2 and $4 than it is between $1 and $2.

FIGURE 1.8

Poverty Incidence at Alternative Poverty Lines, Late 1990s

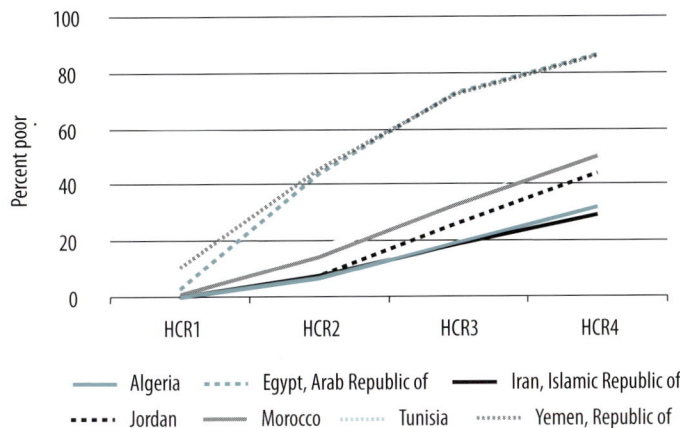

Source: World Bank Global Poverty Monitoring Database.

Note: HCR head count ratio, at $1, $2, $3, and $4.

To give a sense of the size of the poverty challenge in the region, we report in table 1.5 estimates of the number of poor people in 2001 by country at the $2 and $3 poverty lines. As can be seen, even at the $2 line, the scale of the poverty challenge is substantial in Egypt and the Republic of Yemen and is significant in Algeria, the Islamic Republic of Iran, and Morocco. Only in Jordan and Tunisia, having smaller populations to begin with, do the poor number less than a million. The poverty population of the seven data-reporting countries in the region was almost 52 million people (at the $2 line) in 2001. By way of comparison, the number of poor at the $2 line in 1987 was 40 million.

Poverty Characteristics: Evidence from National Poverty Lines

Household survey data make it possible to investigate the relationship between poverty and other household characteristics for which information is typically available: geographic location of the household and the education, employment, occupation, and gender of the head of household. Sometimes information on sources of income is also available, but this is generally considered less robust. We discuss below the broad patterns that can be seen in an overview of poverty characteristics across the region, with the caveat that not all patterns are equally prominent in each country. The link between poverty and education and health is dealt with in later chapters.

Poverty and Location

Three observations may be made with respect to the link between poverty and location on the basis of analysis of Middle East and North Africa

TABLE 1.5

Number of Poor People at Alternative Poverty Lines, 1987 and 2001

Country	Number at $2/Day (millions)		Number at $3/Day (millions)	
	1987	2001	1987	2001
Algeria	2.3	5.1	6.4	11.2
Arab Republic of Egypt	24.2	28.6	38.0	47.6
Islamic Republic of Iran	7.0	3.5	13.9	10.1
Jordan	0.1	0.3	0.3	1.1
Morocco	3.0	4.1	7.8	9.5
Tunisia	1.3	0.5	2.7	1.7
Republic of Yemen	2.2	9.5	4.4	14.1
Total	40.1	51.6	73.5	95.3

Source: World Bank Global Poverty Monitoring Database.

data. First, there is a clear pattern of poverty rates being higher in rural areas than in urban areas. Second, there is also a clear pattern of some regions being relatively poorer than other regions. Nevertheless, and third, where sufficient data are available and have been analyzed, more complex patterns may also be detected where pockets of high poverty coexist with low poverty in both urban and rural areas and within geographic regions.

The first point, regarding the higher rate of poverty in rural areas, can be seen clearly in figure 1.9. For each of the countries in the chart, rural poverty rates are higher. In terms of scale, with the exception of the Republic of Yemen, urban poverty rates are nowhere greater than 15 percent when measured at national poverty lines toward the end of the 1990s. On the other hand, rural poverty rates are uniformly greater than 20 percent, except in Jordan and Tunisia.

The second point, regarding geographic concentrations of poverty, is also observed in several countries in the Middle East and North Africa. To take only two examples, in Tunisia the Center West region is the poorest, and in Egypt rural Upper Egypt is the poorest. In terms of scale, in Tunisia in 2000 the poverty rate in the Center West region was 11 percent as compared to only 1 percent in metropolitan Tunis. Similarly, in Egypt in 2000 the poverty rate in rural Upper Egypt was 34 percent as compared to only 5 percent in metropolitan areas. Concentrations of poverty in so-called lagging regions are not surprising because all countries of reasonable size and topographic diversity tend to have regions that are especially disadvantaged with respect to economic opportunities by remoteness, climate,

FIGURE 1.9

Rural Versus Urban Poverty Rates, Late 1990s

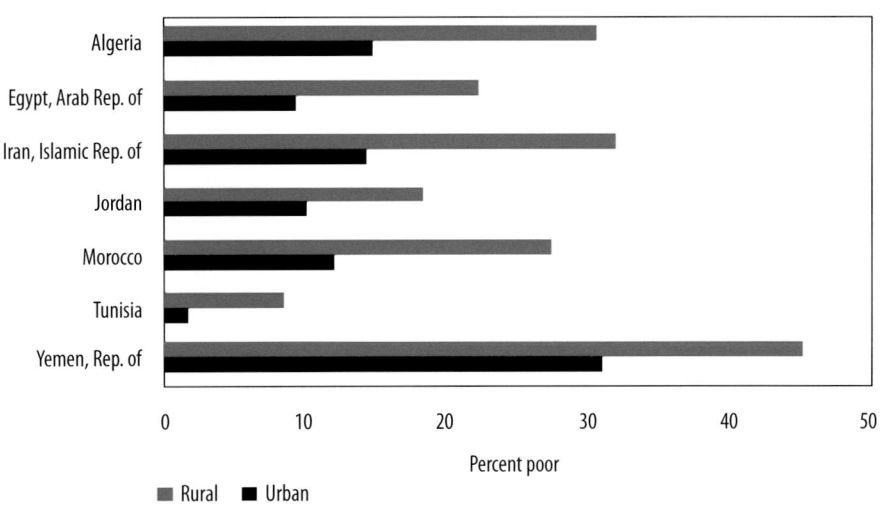

Source: Various World Bank poverty assessments.

soil, or other such factors. Geography, however, is not necessarily destiny. As figure 1.10 shows, sharp changes can also occur in relative ranking over time: in 1990 the poorest region in Tunisia was the North West, but by 2000 poverty had declined dramatically in this region and its position had improved to third-best among Tunisia's six regions (World Bank 2003b).

The third point, regarding greater diversity in poverty patterns at more disaggregated levels, may be illustrated from the case of Morocco. A recent analysis (World Bank 2004e) showed considerable variation in the distribution of poverty among and between regions, provinces, and communes in Morocco. At the most disaggregated level, that of the commune, high concentrations of poverty coexist with low rates, regardless of where the communes are located. This suggests that there may well be efficiency benefits from designing antipoverty programs that can target the commune level. For this to be possible, data have to be collected and analyzed at a suitably disaggregated level. Unfortunately, such analysis has not been done so far for any of the countries in the Middle East and North Africa Region, except Morocco.

Poverty and Employment

The link between employment and poverty extends across three dimensions: sector of employment, nature of occupation, and status of employment. With regard to the sector of employment, the chance of being poor is typically higher for those in the private sector and much lower if one were employed in the public sector. For occupation or nature of economic activity, the chance of being poor is typically highest for those in

FIGURE 1.10

Poverty Incidence by Region in Tunisia, 1990 and 2000

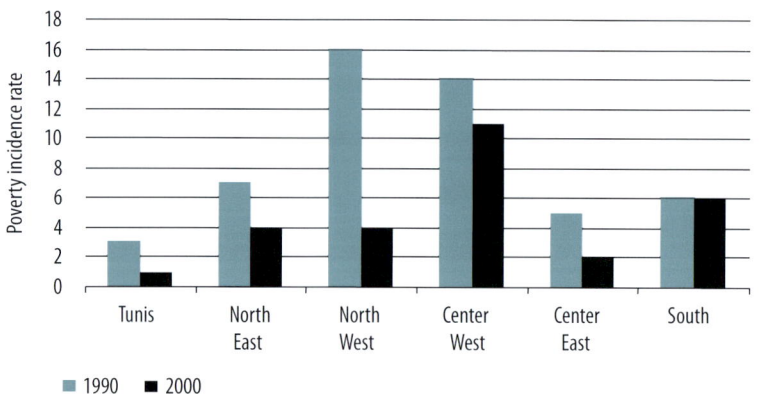

Source: World Bank 2003b.

agriculture and much lower for those in manufacturing or services. Finally, with regard to work status, unpaid workers are more likely to be poor than are paid or self-employed workers, but being unemployed does not necessarily raise the probability of being poor. These patterns are illustrated in figure 1.11 for the case of Egypt in 1999/2000.

The first relationship suggests that one can escape poverty if one is able to get a public sector job. Although this link may be stronger in Egypt, where as much as 28 percent of the labor force was employed in the public sector in 1999/2000, it holds in other countries of the region as well. Unfortunately, this path of escape from poverty is not a sustainable one. Fiscal pressures forced some governments in the region to cut public sector employment rolls and others to freeze hiring levels during the 1990s. The second relationship, between being poor and being in agriculture, is widely observed across the developing world. Agriculture continues to be a lagging sector with comparatively low income growth and high susceptibility to adverse weather and international terms of trade shocks. The third link suggests that the unemployed are not more likely to be poorer than the employed. It is not job status but the income derived from work that determines poverty status. Those who are poor cannot afford to be unemployed and are forced to find work, even of a temporary and casual nature, to make ends meet. On the other hand, a large fraction of the unemployed are often school and college graduates, usually from nonpoor households that can support them financially while they wait for an appropriate job to come along. Also, in some cases, the unemployed may be helped by transfers from family and friends to avoid falling into poverty. The role of transfers is taken up in the next section.

FIGURE 1.11

Poverty and Employment in the Arab Republic of Egypt, 1999/2000

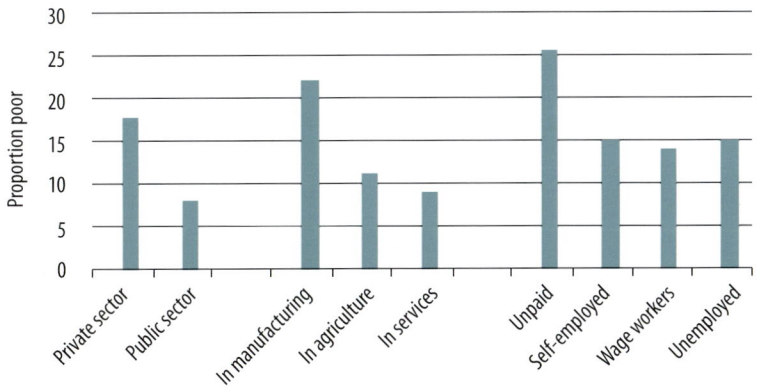

Source: World Bank 2004b.

Poverty and Transfers

It is important to get a sense of the significance of transfers to poverty in order to appreciate how and to what extent social safety nets are working. For example, if public transfers are seen to be very important sources of income for poor households, one could argue that cash transfer programs are effective in reaching the poor, even if they might be inefficient in the sense of leaking to the nonpoor as well. Similarly, if private transfers are an important source of relief for the poor, this provides information about the effectiveness of private safety nets. It was noted earlier that at the macro level remittances appear to have played a statistically significant role in reducing poverty in the Middle East and North Africa, relative to other regions. Can this be verified at the micro level as well?[6]

Data on transfers as a share of income or expenditure of the poor are reported in some of the poverty assessments available for the region. In Egypt, transfers from public and private sources combined amount to around 10 percent of the income of the poor in 1999/2000 (World Bank 2004b). In Jordan, transfers made up 20 percent of the income of the poor in 2002 (World Bank 2004d). In Morocco, transfers account for almost 44 percent of the expenditures of the poorest quintile. Such transfers are made up of roughly equal shares from public and private sources (24 percent and 20 percent, respectively). In the Republic of Yemen, transfers account for just over 38 percent of the expenditures of the poorest decile, but decline to much smaller proportions for higher-income deciles (see figure 1.12). For the poorest rural decile, transfers amount to more than half the level of expenditures.

Surprisingly, the measured impact of private transfers on poverty is higher in Egypt than in Morocco. Poverty in Egypt would have been approxi-

FIGURE 1.12

Public and Private Transfers as a Proportion of Expenditures in the Republic of Yemen

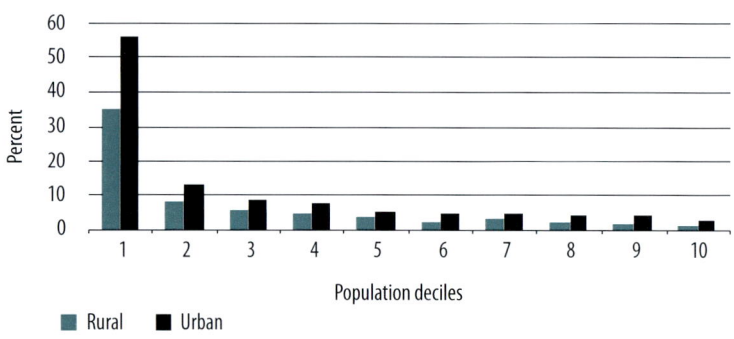

Source: World Bank 2002f.

mately 5 percent higher without private transfers, whereas in Morocco it would have been about 3.4 percent higher. Trying to disentangle the effect of remittances from other transfers is rendered difficult by the fact that none of the available assessments distinguishes clearly among various sources of private transfers.[7] Some indirect information is available in the case of the Republic of Yemen in 1998. It shows that as much as 56 percent of the population living in the poorest decile received some remittances (van de Walle 2002), so this must have been an important source of income for them.

Poverty and Gender

Poverty assessments for several countries in the Middle East and North Africa Region show that female-headed households are *not* likely to be poorer than male-headed households at the national level.[8] For example, in Egypt in 1999/2000 the national poverty rate was 17 percent for male-headed households and 14.6 percent for female-headed households. In other cases, such as Jordan in 2002/03, the level of poverty was higher in female-headed households (15 percent versus 14 percent for male-headed households), but the difference was not statistically significant. Looking at the data another way, in Tunisia in 2000 female heads of households were not overrepresented among the poor: they were 13.2 percent among the poor and 12.3 percent among the nonpoor.[9]

The lack of gender differences in poverty rates at the national level may, in some cases, mask statistically significant differences between rural and urban areas or among geographic regions. For example, in the Islamic Republic of Iran in 1998, gender was a factor in rural areas (where poverty is

FIGURE 1.13

Ratio of Poor Female-Headed to Male-Headed Households by Region in the Arab Republic of Egypt, 1999–2000

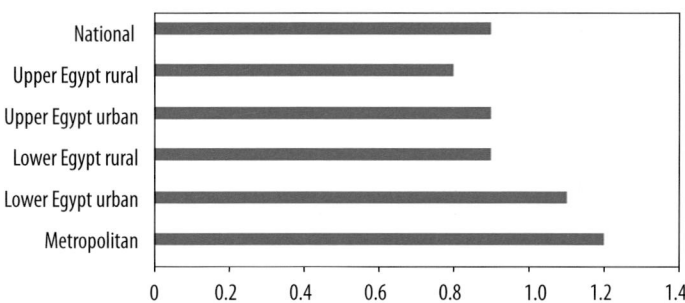

Source: World Bank 2002a.

10 percentage points higher for female-headed households), but not a factor in urban areas. A similar situation prevailed in Tunisia, except that gender there was a factor in urban areas but not so much in rural areas: around 11.8 percent of the population living in female-headed households in rural areas was poor in 2000 as compared to 17.2 percent in urban areas.

Differences in gender-specific poverty rates by geographic region are notable in the case of Egypt. As shown in figure 1.13, the ratio of poor female-headed households to poor male-headed households ranged from 1.2 in metropolitan areas (big cities) to 0.8 in the rural areas of Upper Egypt.

Notes

1. The World Bank Global Poverty Monitoring Data Base can be accessed at http://iresearch.worldbank.org/PovcalNet. It does not necessarily contain information from all surveys done in Middle Eastern and North African countries. For example, Adams and Page (2003) reported national poverty line estimates from a household survey for 1980–81 but this is not in the World Bank's poverty database.
2. On the technical deficiencies of the 1992 Republic of Yemen household survey, see World Bank (2002f), box 1.
3. The comparison here does not include the Europe and Central Asia region, which was not considered part of the set of developing countries during the 1980s.
4. The regional poverty trends shown in figures 1.1 and 1.2 are based on population-weighted averages for the seven countries listed in table 1.1. They were calculated for the years shown by an estimation procedure used as the World Bank and described in appendix.
5. The country-specific trends shown in figure 1.3 are based on actual data for years in which surveys were conducted and on estimates for years in which surveys were not available. The estimates were made using the procedure described in appendix 1.
6. The scale and importance of noncash transfers, such as food and energy subsidies, are discussed in chapter 5.
7. It is difficult to find good micro-level data on the importance of remittances to the poor in the region. Adams (1991) provides some relevant information but this is based on small samples from a few villages rather than from representative national household surveys. The Government of Morocco and the World Bank are currently conducting a survey on migration and remittances in Morocco to see how much remittances contribute to the income of the poor.
8. Data organized by the gender of the head of household do not necessarily provide a perfect basis for detecting gender differences in consumption poverty because the bulk of such differences could well occur within households. However, Egyptian data, disaggregated at the level of individuals rather than households, suggest that this is not the case there: broadly similar proportions of individual males and females (17.1 percent and 16.3 percent, respectively) were found to be poor in 1999/2000.
9. One reason for the economic resilience of female-headed households may be the fact that the husband is working abroad and sending remittances. Migration and remittances are known to be important in each of the three countries cited here.

CHAPTER 2

Trends in Human Development Indicators

To the extent that development should be thought of as not just a change in incomes but also a change in capabilities that improves and expands the control of poor people over their lives, it is important to look at human development indicators side by side with income or consumption measures. Information on trends in human development indicators can supplement the information obtained from consumption-based surveys for a better understanding of poverty performance. In particular, such information can provide additional texture to the poverty results by showing how changes in income or consumption are reflected in such tangible outcomes as, say, child mortality or school enrollment.

Regional Comparisons

A summary overview of changes in such human development indicators as education attainment, female education attainment, child mortality, and life expectancy shows remarkable progress in the Middle East and North Africa Region between 1960 and 2000.[1] In these four decades, years of education for people age 15 and above rose sixfold, years of education for females (age 15 and above) rose ninefold, and child mortality fell more than fivefold; life expectancy rose by 44 percent (see table 2.1).

To place this progress in perspective we need to compare the region's performance with that of other countries. Most international comparisons are done among countries falling within similar income groups (such as low income, lower-middle income, upper-middle income, and so on). We have developed a set of comparators by choosing countries that fell within the same range of per capita incomes (in PPP terms) as did the Middle Eastern and North African countries in 1980. The 30 countries thus selected into the comparator group had a population-weighted mean income of $11.29 per capita per day, whereas the Middle East and North Africa group (MENA10) had a mean income of $11.17 per capita per day.

TABLE 2.1

Human Development in the Middle East and North Africa, Selected years, 1960–2000

Indicator	1960	1980	2000
Years of education (average per person over 15)	0.9	2.6	5.5
Years of education (average per female over 15)	0.5	1.8	4.6
Child mortality (deaths per 1,000 births)	262	138	47
Life expectancy (years expected at birth)	47	58	68

Sources: World Development Indicators, CD-ROM 2004; and World Bank EdStats, www.worldbank.org/education/edstats.

The comparator group mostly comprises presently middle-income and lower-middle-income countries from Latin America and East Asia (see appendix 2 for a list of the comparator countries).

The comparison shown in the four panels of figure 2.1 is quite favorable to MENA10. In each area of comparison, MENA10 started with a worse level of the indicator of interest in 1960 but ended in 2000 by having substantially narrowed the gap with the comparator group (as in years of education for all and for females) or even having eliminated it (as for child mortality and life expectancy).

By subperiod, the relevant indicators show a pattern that is different from that observed in the case of poverty. Whereas poverty reduction effectively stalled after the mid-1980s, there is no such break for the human development indicators, which show substantial improvement in both subperiods (1960–80 and 1980–2000). This is surprising in view of the fact that economic growth was so much slower for the Middle East and North Africa during 1980–2000 than in the 20 years before (see figure 2.2). The region's performance is similarly surprising when viewed in comparative terms. Whereas its per capita income path *diverged* dramatically from that of its comparators (see figure 2.2), the region's social indicators *converged* with those of comparators over the period 1980–2000 (see figure 2.1).

It is possible that the superiority of MENA10's performance may be more apparent than real and may be a function of the measure being used for comparison. The simple linear percentage change that is reflected in figure 2.1 may be a misleading measure of policy and effort to the extent that it does not control for the initial level of each indicator nor for resources applied to human development. Adjusting for initial levels is important because these determine how hard it may be to bring about a change in the relevant indicator. For example, if the level of child mortality is already quite low, it will be harder to bring about further reductions than if the level is higher at the outset. Similarly, for countries starting from a very low level, it is likely to be easier to increase the level of female

FIGURE 2.1

Comparative Trends in Human Development Indicators, 1960–2000

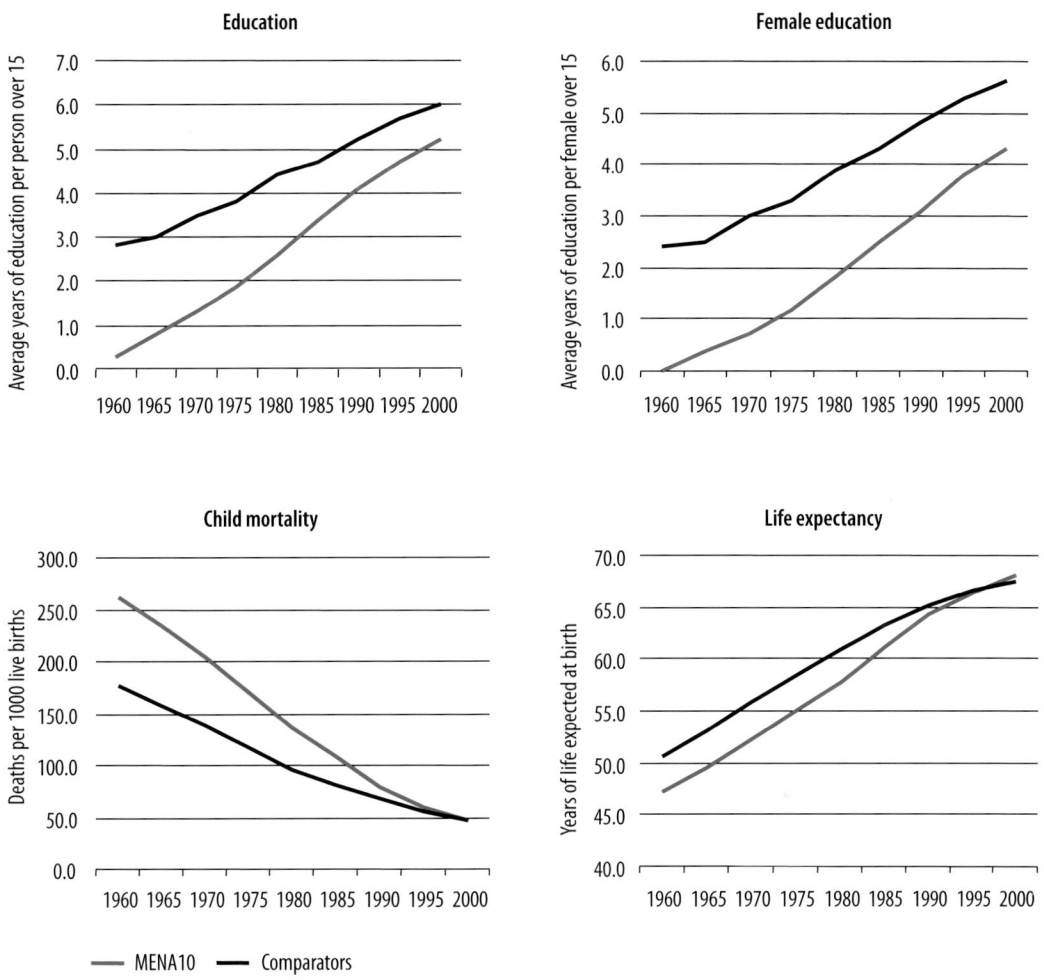

Sources: World Development Indicators, CD-ROM 2004; and World Bank EdStats, www.worldbank.org/education/edstats.

education than it might be for countries that are already much farther ahead on this score. Adjusting for resource application is also important because countries that grow faster and/or devote higher levels of resources to improving social indicators should show better results.

Country-Specific Performance

The figures in this section show the comparative performance of individual MENA10 countries for several indicators when the above-mentioned adjustments are made. Specifically, we have estimated econometric equa-

FIGURE 2.2

Per Capita GDP Trajectories, 1960–2000

(PPP dollars per day)

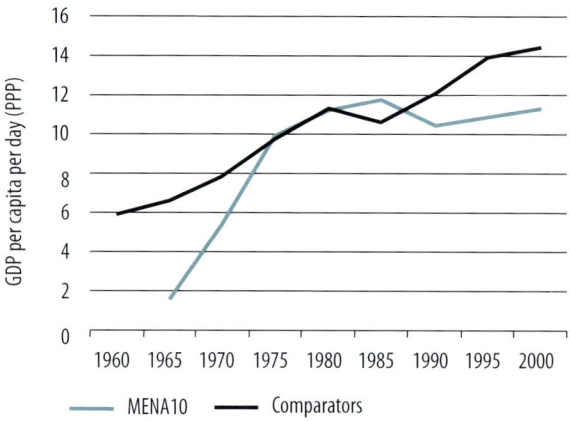

Source: Staff calculations.

Note: MENA10 includes Algeria, the Arab Republic of Egypt, the Islamic Republic of Iran, Jordan, Lebanon, Libya, Morocco, Syria, Tunisia, and the Republic of Yemen.

tions for the year 2000 where the dependent variable is the change in social indicator between 1980 and 2000 and the independent variables are initial income in 1980; initial level of indicator in 1980; growth of income per capita between 1980 and 2000; and average level of education spending per capita during 1980–2000. The last-mentioned variable is used as a proxy for a country's stance with respect to social spending. The charts show the extent to which each country exceeds or is below the indicator level that would have been predicted for it (in the year 2000) on the basis of the econometric model.

The results are striking. They show that most MENA10 countries for which suitable data are available have performed better than predicted on the basis of the four determinants used and better than most comparator countries across all selected indicators.

Educational Attainment (All)

Five of the eight Middle Eastern and North African countries for which we have data on this variable have performed better than expected, and three have performed worse than expected (see figure 2.3). The Republic of Yemen has been the star overperformer, whereas Tunisia has been a notable underperformer. Tunisia's performance should be viewed in the context of two observations. First, the rating applies to performance compared with prediction and so is a relative concept; in absolute terms, of

FIGURE 2.3

Comparative Performance in Mean Years of Education, 2000

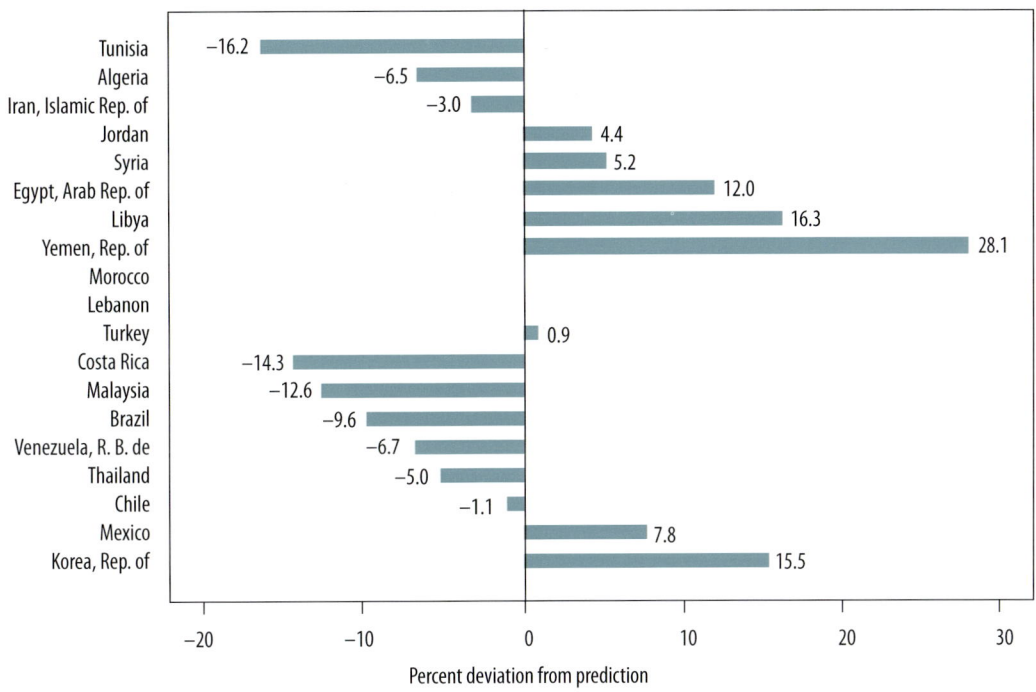

Source: Staff calculations.

course, Tunisia has one of the region's better records in education. Second, Tunisia had higher income growth and education spending than other countries in the region during the last two decades; accordingly, a higher performance bar had to be met. The weaker-than-expected performance may reflect inefficiencies in Tunisia's education delivery system.[2]

Educational Attainment (Females)

The performance of Middle Eastern and North African countries is especially impressive in the case of improvements in number of years of education for females. For a region that is supposed to have substantial cultural obstacles to female education, its relative performance is remarkable. Not only did most of the countries perform better than expected with respect to female education during 1980–2000; they also outperformed many comparators in East Asia and Latin America (see figure 2.4). Indeed, Egypt, Libya, and the Republic of Yemen outperformed all comparators in the set.

FIGURE 2.4

Comparative Performance in Mean Years of Female Education, 2000

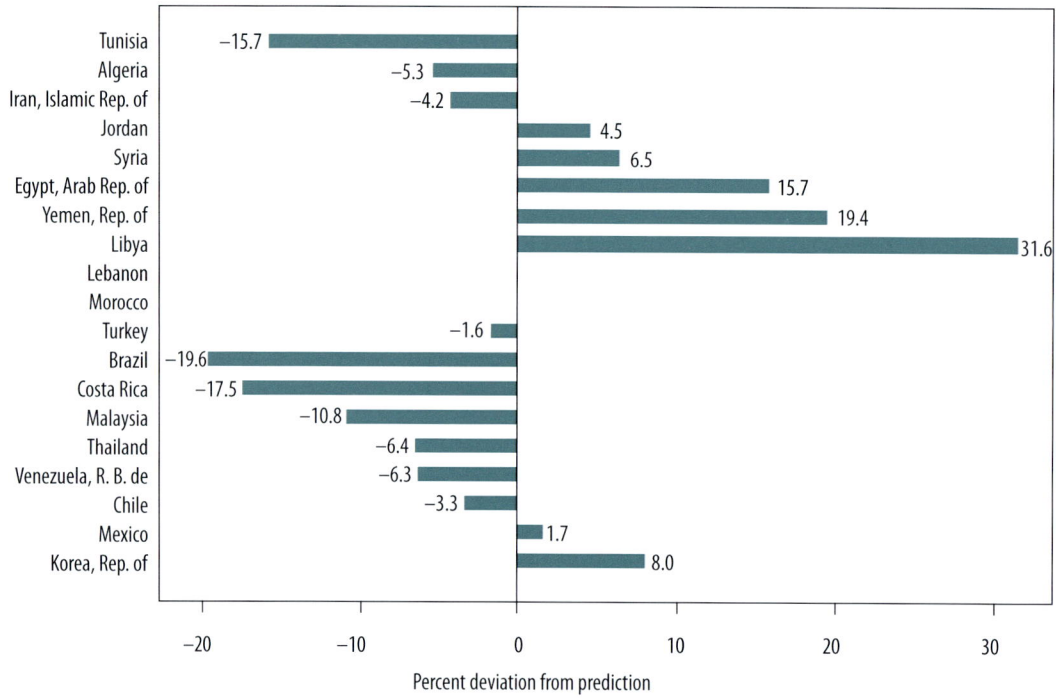

Percent deviation from prediction

Source: Staff calculations.

Child Mortality

Nine of the region's 10 countries for which child mortality data are available show better-than-expected results (see figure 2.5). Performance has been exceptionally good in countries such as Egypt, Libya, Morocco, and Syria, and relatively good in Algeria, Tunisia, and the Republic of Yemen. The only country that appears to have done less well than expected is Lebanon, perhaps because the country was in a state of conflict during the 1980s and/or possibly because there was a lack of attention paid to public provision of health care. Once again, most Middle Eastern and North African countries are seen to perform better than most comparators (with the exception of Malaysia).

Life Expectancy

The results for life expectancy are similar to those for child mortality. All countries in the region, except Lebanon, have done better than expected in the last two decades and better than all comparators (see figure 2.6). Egypt and the Republic of Yemen stand out in having especially good performance.

FIGURE 2.5

Comparative Performance in Mortality among Children Less than 5 Years of Age, 2000

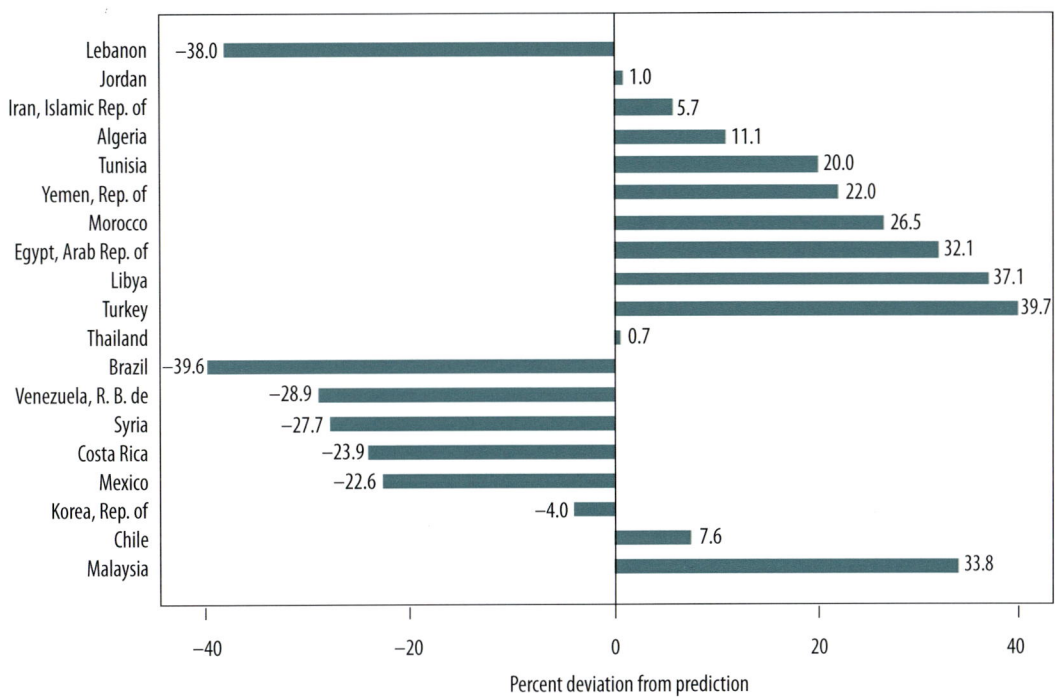

Source: Staff calculations.

The impressive performance of the region, especially after controlling for income and public spending factors, suggests that gains in efficiency in the systems of education and health care delivery must have played an important role. Health gains, in particular, may also have come about from improvements in other areas, such as education (of mothers), access to safe water, access to food subsidies, and enhanced transport infrastructure. It is also possible that education and health gains may have occurred as a consequence of rising private expenditures. These factors are explored in more detail in later chapters on education, health, and social safety nets. For the moment, we take up the gender aspect of human development.

Gender Dimensions of Human Development

Gender may be considered an important aspect of human development to the extent that the health and education of women are important contributors to the living standards of future generations, and women's participation in the

FIGURE 2.6

Comparative Performance in Life Expectancy, 2000

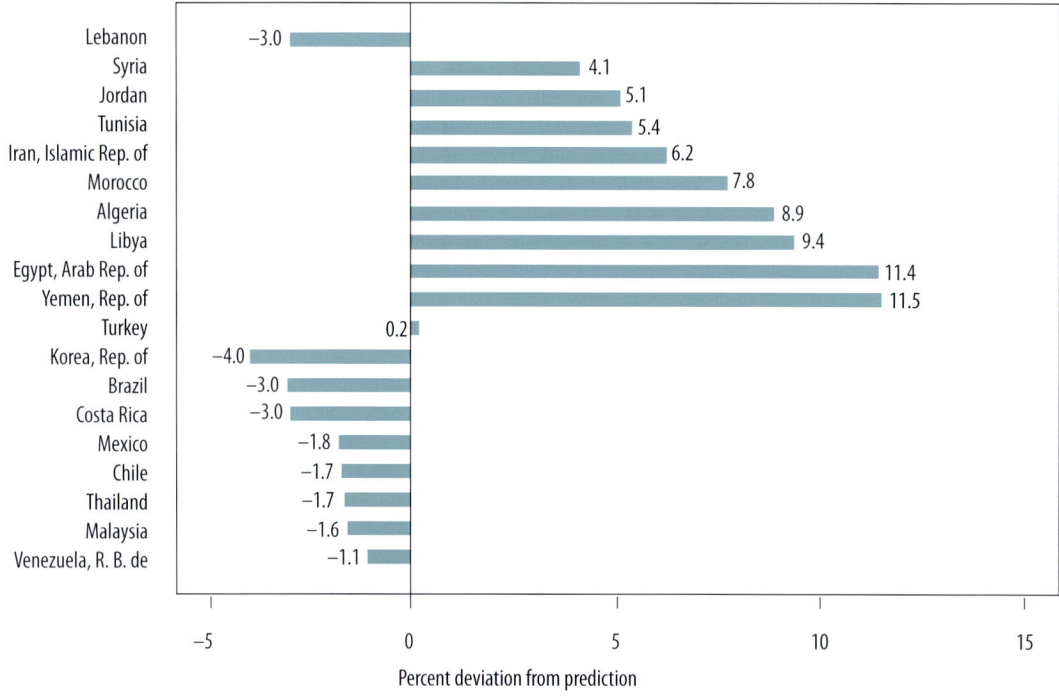

Percent deviation from prediction

Source: Staff calculations.

formal economy is an important determinant of economic growth. In particular, the education of girls has well-documented indirect effects in overcoming poverty at both household and national levels. Aside from the immediate impact on household earnings, educated women marry later and have smaller families with healthier and better-educated children, thus transforming the development capacity of future generations. Accordingly, in this section, we look at some gender-specific indicators of human development. In particular, we document trends in literacy and life expectancy as measures of female education and health, and fertility and labor force participation rates as measures of the degree of autonomy over their life choices and roles achieved by women in the region. We provide only a brief overview of the relevant issues because a detailed discussion is available in *Gender and Development in the Middle East and North Africa: Women in the Public Sphere* (World Bank 2004c).

Trends in Female Literacy

Female literacy trends are shown in figure 2.7. They show that female literacy had risen from less than 10 percent in 1960 to 60 percent by 2000.

Moreover, the rate of change was steady and similar to that of comparator countries until approximately 1990. After 1990 there are signs of convergence with comparators. However, given the large gaps that have persisted in this dimension between MENA10 and its comparators, full convergence is still a long way off. Whereas average female literacy rates are around 60 percent for the region, they are as high as 85 percent among comparators. Another interesting dimension (not shown in the figure) is the one relating to the literacy gap between men and women. Here there is clear evidence of a rapidly equalizing trend. Whereas the ratio of literate females to literate males was only 0.63 in 1980, it had risen to almost 0.87 by 2000. Once again, the rate of progress was faster than among comparator countries.

Trends in Female Life Expectancy

Since 1960 female life expectancy has increased steadily in MENA10 countries, rising from 48 years on average in 1960 to almost 70 years in 2000 (see figure 2.8). By now, the region has the same average female life expectancy rate as comparator countries. The gap between female and male life expectancy also has increased in favor of women in most MENA10 countries, although the gap is still below the five years or so that is observed in most middle-income countries.[3]

Trends in Fertility

Figure 2.9 shows that the Middle East and North Africa Region as a whole has achieved significant reductions in fertility (births per woman aged between 15 and 49 years) over the past four decades. Indeed, the pattern of reduction is remarkable in that, during the period 1980–2000,

FIGURE 2.7

Trends in Female Literacy

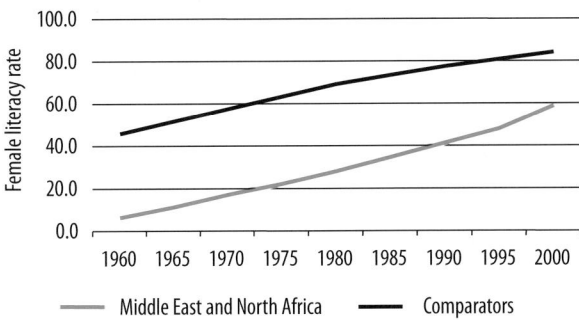

Sources: World Development Indicators, CD-ROM 2004, and staff calculations.

FIGURE 2.8

Trends in Female Life Expectancy

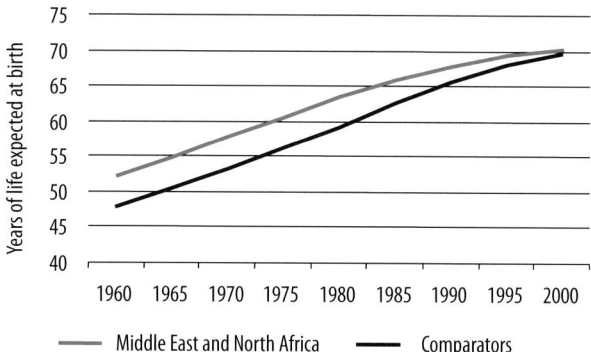

Sources: World Development Indicators, CD-ROM 2004, and staff calculations.

FIGURE 2.9

Trends in Fertility

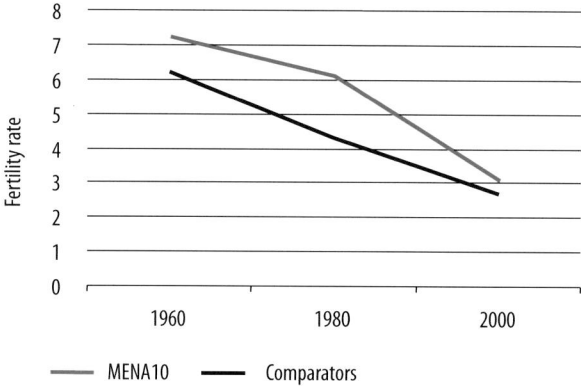

Sources: World Development Indicators, CD-ROM 2004, and staff calculations.

Note: MENA10 includes Algeria, the Arab Republic of Egypt, the Islamic Republic of Iran, Jordan, Lebanon, Libya, Morocco, Syria, Tunisia, and the Republic of Yemen.

the pace was faster than among comparators, to the extent that average fertility levels are now almost at par with those among comparators—and this despite the fact that in the two decades between 1960 and 1980 the gap with comparators actually had widened.

Trends in Labor Force Participation

The Middle East and North Africa Region appears to have made rapid gains in rates of female labor force participation (see figure 2.10). From a situation where only about a fifth of the female labor force (21.9 percent)

FIGURE 2.10

Trends in Female Labor Force Participation

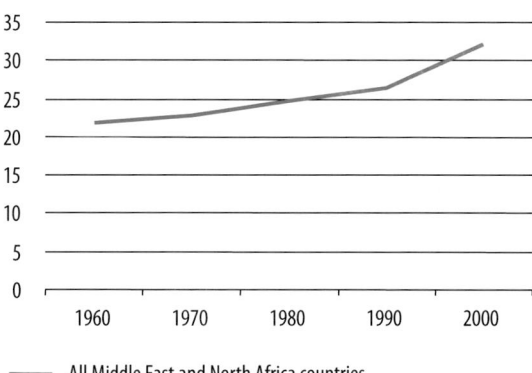

——— All Middle East and North Africa countries

Sources: World Development Indicators, CD-ROM 2004, and staff calculations.

was participating in the formal economy in 1960, the region now has a participation rate of almost a third (32.2 percent). The pattern of change over time shows the bulk of the increase as having occurred in the last decade: the participation rate climbed as much between 1990 and 2000 as in the previous three decades between 1960 and 1990. However, it also should be noted that, despite the increase in recent decades, the level of participation in MENA10 countries remains far below that of regions with much lower per capita incomes, such as Sub-Saharan Africa (62.5 percent) and South Asia (46.5 percent).

We must once again ask the question, are these patterns of rapid change an accurate measure of performance? And, as before, one way to measure performance is to compare the actual change over time with what would have been predicted on the basis of some reasonable determinants. An exercise carried out along these lines and reported in World Bank (2004c) shows that, in the case of female labor force participation, the performance of the Middle East and North Africa Region was less than might have been expected on the basis of changes in its fertility rates, female education levels, and age profile. So on this dimension of human development, we must conclude that the "potential to integrate women into the regional economy, determined by past investment in female education and recent fertility trends, has not been realized" (World Bank 2004c, p. 62).

Notes

1. MENA10 in this chapter refers to the following 10 countries for which data on social indicators since 1960 were available: Algeria, Egypt, the Islamic Re-

public of Iran, Jordan, Lebanon, Libya, Morocco, Syria, Tunisia, and the Republic of Yemen. For the education variables used in table 2.1, data were not available for Lebanon and Morocco.

2. Because data on years of education completed were not available for Lebanon and Morocco, we have checked these countries' performance by running regressions using gross secondary enrollment change (between 1980 and 2000) as the dependent variable. Seven of the MENA10 countries in the sample do better than expected (including Lebanon) and three do worse (including Morocco).

3. Maternal mortality is another relevant dimension here. Unfortunately, data on this are limited to the 1990s. According to a recent report by the United Nations Development Programme, only two Arab countries (Kuwait and the United Arab Emirates) have maternal mortality rates that are low by international standards of five or less per 100,000 live births (UNDP 2002, p. 40). Nevertheless, this is also an area where improvements have occurred among Middle Eastern and North African countries (see World Bank 2004c, p. 161).

CHAPTER 3

Education and Poverty

The Middle East and North Africa Region has a strong record in providing education to its citizens. Chapter 2 of this report has highlighted two notable features of the region's achievements with respect to certain conventional quantitative indicators of educational attainment. First, the region has made gains at a faster rate than its comparators since 1960. Second, during 1980–2000, the region's gains in education have been faster than can be explained by its initial levels of income and education and by its income growth and public spending profile. These findings raise some questions that we attempt to answer in this chapter. The first set of questions applies to the link between education and poverty. Although education attainments have risen on average, has this translated into clear gains in education for poorer income groups? And to what extent has the acquisition of education helped in poverty reduction in the region? A second set of questions pertains to the reasons for the strong performance of the region during the last two decades. Was this because of rising levels of spending on education or because of improvements in the education delivery system? What role did private spending play? A third and final set of questions relates to the quality dimension of education. Gains clearly have been made along conventional quantitative dimensions, but is this true as well of quality? If not, what aspects of the challenge of improving quality have the strongest bearing on poverty reduction in the future?

With regard to the first set of questions, it is clear that, although access to education still may be a problem in some countries, significant gains have accrued to the poor of the region. This is demonstrated by the substantial increases in primary and secondary enrollments that have taken place. What is not easily demonstrable is whether these "access" gains in education have translated into large "income" gains for the poor. Given the high level of unemployment in the region, especially among the educated, it is debatable whether the acquisition of education is an automatic route to employment and higher income. And the limited data that are available on rates of return to education in the region show that these tend to be on the low side, possibly reflecting both poor quality of education and weak labor demand.

With regard to the role of spending on education attainment, we find that public education spending in the Middle East and North Africa Region actually decreased as a share of GDP and on a per capita basis during the 1990s. So the improved performance must reflect other factors, such as efficiency gains in the delivery of education services and increases in private spending. There are anecdotal data to support this view, although they are not strong enough to sustain a firm conclusion.

Finally, with regard to the quality dimension, the information presently available suggests that, although it is not possible to assert that the quality of education declined during the 1990s, it is true that education quality must be improved to cope with the challenges of a more competitive global environment in the future.

Education–Poverty Links

To assess gains for the poor, it is best to look at primary enrollment data. Because the nonpoor typically have close to 100 percent primary enrollment rates, any increase in the average over time is likely to come from disproportionate gains in enrollment among the poor. So an increasing primary enrollment rate provides strong evidence of improving access to education among the poor. The data for this region are very clear in this regard. As figure 3.1 shows, gross primary enrollment has risen rapidly in all countries of the region since 1970. Indeed, it has been above 95 percent since 1990. Furthermore, enrollment rates have been rising steadily for secondary schooling as well; this is also likely to reflect rising rates of access for the poor.

Evidence of rising education levels among the poor is also available from some country-specific household surveys. Examples from some recent surveys analyzed by World Bank staff include Egypt, where 23 percent of the poor population had basic education and 12 percent had secondary education in 1999/2000, compared with 21 percent and 10 percent, respectively, in 1995–96 (World Bank 2004b); and Jordan, where illiteracy among the poor dropped from 22 percent in 1997 to 13 percent in 2002 (World Bank 2004d). More direct evidence on the improving access of the poor to education was provided in a recent study for Morocco (World Bank 2004e). The correlation between primary enrollment rates and provincial-level poverty was checked at two points in time, 1994 and 2001. It was discovered that provinces with higher poverty rates had higher enrollments per capita in 2004, whereas the reverse had been true in 1994. The percentage change in enrollment rates also was found to be

FIGURE 3.1

Trends in Gross Enrollments in the Middle East and North Africa Region, 1970–2000

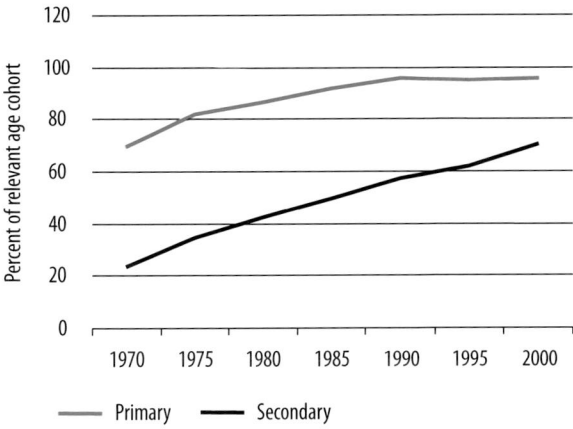

Source: World Bank EdStats, www.worldbank.org/education/edstats.

higher in initially poorer provinces. Both these facts point to a catching up of enrollment rates in poorer provinces over time.

Remaining Access Challenges

Despite substantial improvements in access to education over the past four decades, challenges on this front remain in some countries. In particular, the issue of access remains critical in the Republic of Yemen where, despite extraordinary recent progress, less than 60 percent of children complete primary education. In some countries the remaining challenges are more in the nature of geographic pockets of low access. For example, although illiteracy has declined steadily throughout Egypt, 52 percent of the poor in rural Upper Egypt remain illiterate. Groups who are still excluded throughout the region, or who drop out before completing primary education, are typically the poor and girls in remote rural areas, the disabled in all income groups, and working and street children in urban areas.

The constraints to access of the poor and girls in rural areas include distance to school and the direct and indirect user costs of schooling. Dropping out of school is attributed to increasing opportunity costs for the poor as children get older, to lack of acceptable facilities and security for girls, and to perceived poor quality and low value of the education provided. Measures to overcome these constraints to participation of the poor and of girls include focusing resources on school facilities and inputs in poor rural communities; targeting subsidies conditional on school attendance for the very poor and for girls; community participation in school decisions; subsidies and incentives for secondary and tertiary education; adapting curricula to local needs; media/public information campaigns on inclusion of girls and disabled and vulnerable groups; and programs to mainstream disabled people, street children, and orphans.

Education and Income Growth among Poor People

Most poverty assessments find a high correlation between education status and income status. The Middle East and North Africa Region is no exception to this general pattern. In all cases where detailed analysis of household data has been carried out, poverty rates are highest for households headed by illiterate people and decline with increased education of the household head. In Egypt, for example, the chance of being poor was found to drop from 24 percent for the illiterate to 2 percent for those with university education (see figure 3.2). In the Republic of Yemen, households whose head had completed primary education were 18 percent less likely to be poor than were those households with illiterate heads.

Clearly, poverty is inversely correlated with education attainment. But are well-off people better educated because they can afford education, or are they better off because they are well educated? Tracing the impact of education in poverty reduction is complex because of the interaction of the factors involved and because of the time lag in realizing many of the benefits. By looking more closely at the channels through which education reduces poverty, however, we can throw some light on the factors

FIGURE 3.2

Poverty and Education Attainment in Selected Countries
(Percent)

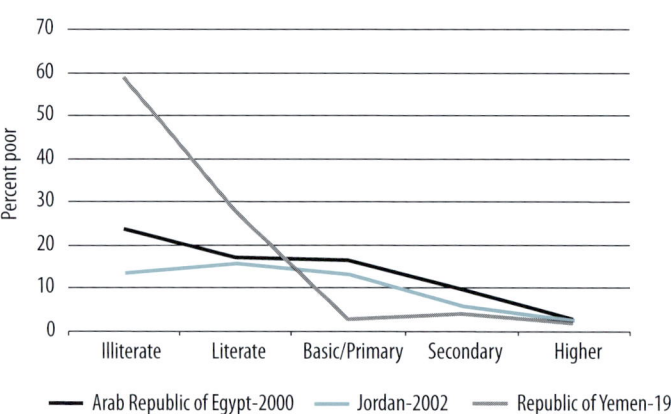

Sources: World Bank 2004b, 2004d, and 2002f for the Arab Republic of Egypt, Jordan, and the Republic of Yemen, respectively.

that have been constraining or enhancing its impact in the Middle East and North Africa.

Education can help a family climb out of poverty directly by increasing household income, through increasing the productivity of self-employed workers, or by enabling access to higher-paid jobs. Whereas direct measures of the impact of education on the productivity of self-employed workers are not available, a limited amount of information is available for some countries on an indirect measure—the private rate of return on education. A recent analysis (World Bank 2004b) provided estimates for four countries (Egypt, Jordan, Morocco, and the Republic of Yemen) using a common methodology. The results (shown in table 3.1) reflect generally low rates of return on education. In some cases, as for males in public employment, the rates generally fell in the 1990s. For example, in Egypt the rate of return for males in public employment was 8.2 percent for primary education in 1988, and it fell to 6.4 percent by 1998. For Morocco the equivalent rate was 12.4 percent in 1991 and fell to 6.1 percent in 1999. For Jordan and the Republic of Yemen, rates of return are only available for 1997, and they are even lower than those for Egypt and Morocco. By way of comparison, Psacharopoulos and Patrinos (2002) reported average returns on investment in education of 20 percent for Asia, 27 percent for Latin America and the Caribbean, and 38 percent for Sub-Saharan Africa. The general impression from these statistics is that education was not a high-yielding investment in Middle Eastern and North African countries during the 1990s.

Another perspective on this point is available from information on the other channel linking education to income, namely, employment for

TABLE 3.1

Rates of Return on Schooling for Males in Selected Countries, Selected Years

Education Level	Arab Rep. of Egypt 1988	Arab Rep. of Egypt 1998	Morocco 1991	Morocco 1999	Jordan 1997	Rep. of Yemen 1997
Males in public employment						
Primary	8.2	6.4	12.4	6.1	3.5	2.7
Lower secondary	7.0	4.9	10.7	8.2	2.9	2.7
Upper secondary, general	8.6	8.8	10.6	8.8	2.8	2.2
Upper secondary, vocational	9.6	7.2	8.4	6.8	3.8	3.3
University	10.1	8.8	10.8	8.9	4.6	3.8
Males in private employment						
Primary	2.3	3.6	3.0	3.4	2.0	2.7
Lower secondary	2.5	4.4	6.4	6.3	5.5	2.7
Upper secondary, general	6.3	7.3	10.4	7.7	6.0	2.2
Upper secondary, vocational	5.3	5.0	6.9	5.8	3.2	3.3
University	8.5	7.3	12.5	9.5	10.2	5.2

Source: Adapted from World Bank (2004i), table 4.6.

wages. Here the picture is even clearer. The Middle East and North Africa Region has high unemployment rates. These rates rose during the 1980s and 1990s, and are generally higher among the educated parts of the population. Data on unemployment for 12 Middle Eastern and North African countries show that unemployment rose from an average of just over 8 percent of the labor force in 1980 to around 11 percent in 1990 and close to 15 percent in 2000 (World Bank 2004h, figure 1.9).[1] That these rates are high can be confirmed by comparing them with rates in other middle-income countries, which were around 9 percent in 2000—almost 6 points below the Middle Eastern and North African level. Finally, the fact that most of the unemployed tend to be those with primary and secondary education, as opposed to having no education, is shown in figure 3.3.

Education Spending and Poverty Reduction

Trends in Education Spending

Education spending (for all three levels—primary, secondary, and tertiary) in MENA10 countries shows a very clear two-part trend since 1965 (see figure 3.4). In the first part, between 1965 and 1980, education spending per capita rose more than fivefold, from less than $50 to more than $250 (corresponding roughly to an increase in the ratio of spending to GDP from 4 percent to 6.5 percent). At this level, MENA10 countries not only were spending more on education than their middle-income

FIGURE 3.3

Distribution of Jobseekers by Level of Education

(Percent)

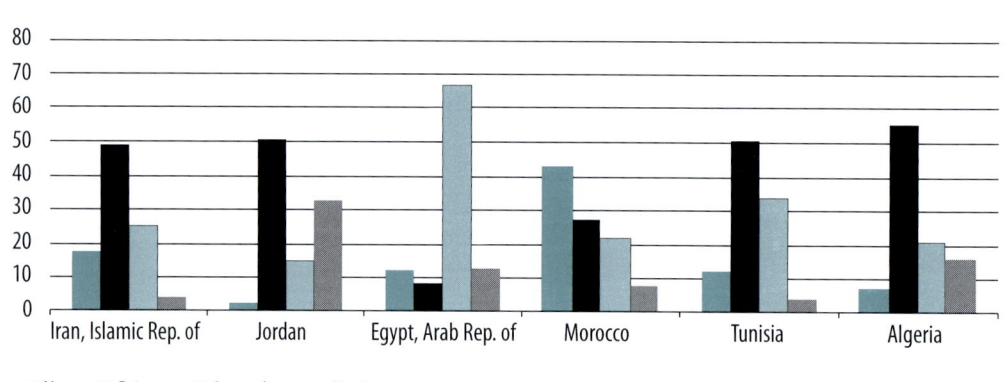

Source: Adapted from World Bank 2004i, figure 4.4.

comparators, but also spending more than Organisation for Economic Co-operation and Development countries on average. The second part of the trend, between 1980 and 2000, shows a sharp decline in the 1980s and a slow rise during the 1990s such that the level of spending was just below $200 per capita by the year 2000. The first phase of the trend helps explain the region's strong performance in raising education attainments prior to 1980. The second phase suggests that the region's continued strong performance in education attainment since 1980 must have been due in part to other sources, including improvements in the efficiency of the education delivery system.

Country-level disaggregation of spending patterns reveals some other notable aspects. For example, in recent years the country that has been spending the most on education is the Republic of Yemen (see table 3.2). Indeed, at 9.9 percent of GDP, that country is spending three times the average for low-income economies. Lebanon, a country with high attainments, spends very little public money on education (around 2 percent in 1999/2000); this is largely because, alone among countries in the region, Lebanon has a well-developed and active private education system and the bulk of spending is done there. Between 60 and 70 percent of primary enrollments are in private schools.

The poverty impact of public spending on education depends in part on its incidence among income groups. *The benefit incidence of expenditure on education in the Middle East and North Africa Region follows the typical pattern of being pro-poor at the basic level, and pro-rich at the tertiary level.* Because the poor tend to drop out of the education system earlier than the

FIGURE 3.4

Trends in Education Spending Per Capita, 1960–2000

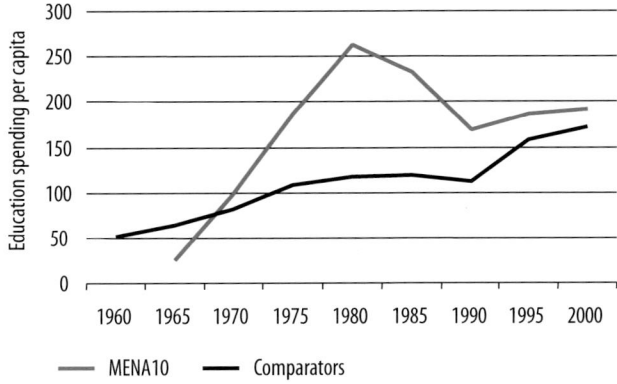

Source: World Bank EdStats, www.worldbank.org/education/edstats.

Note: MENA10 includes Algeria, the Arab Republic of Egypt, the Islamic Republic of Iran, Jordan, Lebanon, Libya, Morocco, Syria, Tunisia, and the Republic of Yemen.

TABLE 3.2

Country-Specific Patterns of Public Education Spending, Selected Years, 1970–2000
(Percent of GDP)

Country	1970	1975	1980	1985	1990	1995	1999–2000
Algeria	7.72	6.64	7.60	8.32	5.31	5.43	—
Arab Republic of Egypt	4.74	5.03	—	5.67	3.89	4.67	—
Islamic Republic of Iran	—	—	7.51	3.65	4.08	4.08	4.94
Jordan	3.81	3.83	6.79	6.79	8.06	8.23	4.95
Lebanon	—	—	—	—	—	2.73	2.08
Morocco	3.47	5.21	5.89	5.94	5.27	5.60	6.07
Syria	3.85	3.95	4.58	6.08	4.00	3.18	—
Tunisia	6.81	5.03	5.24	5.54	5.99	6.48	7.54
Republic of Yemen	—	—	—	—	—	4.49	9.90

Source: World Bank EdStats, www.worldbank.org/education/edstats.

Note: — Not available.

less poor, and are much less likely to continue to the tertiary level of education, expenditure at the tertiary level inevitably favors those who are better off. This is illustrated by figure 3.5, which shows how the distribution of educational subsidies varies among income groups for different levels of education in Jordan: the bottom quintile receives three times the subsidy for basic education (30 percent) that it receives for higher education (only 10 percent), whereas for the top quintile, the ratio is reversed. Similar patterns are found in other countries as well. In Tunisia the poorest 10 percent received more than twice as much of the education subsidy at the primary level as the richest 10 percent in 1990. Conversely, the richest 10 percent of the population received three times as much subsidy as the poorest 10 percent at the secondary level, and 20 times as much in higher education. In Morocco approximately 25 percent of the subsidy for primary education goes to the poorest quintile and 10 percent to the richest quintile; these proportions are reversed for secondary education, and for tertiary education more than 40 percent of the subsidy flows to the richest quintile.

Have education spending biases increased or declined over time in the Middle East and North Africa? We can attempt to answer this question by looking at trends in the budget shares of different levels of education. Unfortunately, the data at hand do not allow for a decisive opinion on this point. The only category for which a satisfactory time series exists is tertiary education. With respect to tertiary education, it would appear that budget shares have been constant or have risen since the mid-1980s (see table 3.3). So it is unlikely that more funds have been found for primary and secondary schooling from the reallocation of existing education budgets away from tertiary spending. Furthermore, in most cases tertiary education shares in Middle Eastern and North African countries contin-

FIGURE 3.5

Benefit Incidence of Public Education Spending: Jordan, 2002

(Percent)

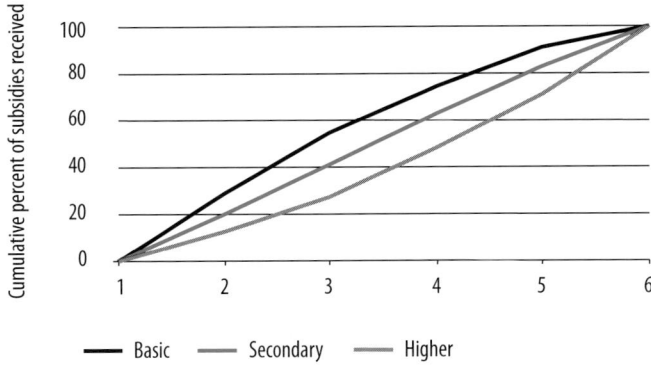

— Basic   — Secondary   — Higher

Source: World Bank 2004d.

TABLE 3.3

Expenditure Shares on Tertiary Education, Selected Years, 1980–2000

(Percentage of total spending on education)

Country	1980	1985	1990	1995	2000
Algeria	11.55	—	—	—	—
Arab Republic of Egypt	—	—	31.09	32.6	—
Islamic Republic of Iran	6.23	9.47	11.21	19.01	19.38
Jordan	15.22	24.28	24.83	24.44	—
Lebanon	—	—	—	17.29	—
Morocco	14.79	13.54	14.74	—	—
Syria	26.29	27.98	21.34	—	—
Tunisia	17.91	16.41	16.21	16.36	21.65
Lower-middle-income average	14.55	16.42	15.85	16.34	17.8

Source World Bank EdStats, www.worldbank.org/education/edstats.
Note: — Not available.

ue to be higher than the average (around 18 percent) for lower-middle-income countries.

A complementary perspective can be obtained by looking at the efficiency with which available funds are used at different levels of education. Once again the data on which to base an opinion are effectively limited to the tertiary sector. Expenditures per tertiary student, measured as a percentage of per capita GDP, have declined in the Islamic Republic of Iran, Jordan, Morocco, and Tunisia since 1985 (see table 3.4). These trends may reflect some efficiency gains but also could indicate overcrowding and deteriorating services. If the latter interpretation is more accurate,

TABLE 3.4

Public Expenditure Per Tertiary Student, Selected Years, 1980–2002

(Percent of per capita GDP)

Country	1980	1985	1995	2000	2002
Arab Republic of Egypt	54.08	—	—	—	—
Islamic Republic of Iran	—	88.19	43.6	38.04	33.46
Jordan	61.68	81.08	85.2	32.1	—
Lebanon	—	—	23.14	8.19	—
Morocco	150.34	96.18	—	110.88	94.62
Syria	74.74	98.55	—	—	—
Tunisia	188.09	158.68	84.33	67.99	53.62
Lower middle income	92.84	93.17	44.72	71.99	63.27

Source: World Bank EdStats, www.worldbank.org/education/edstats.

Note: — Not available.

then the nominal efficiencies may have come at a potential cost to future labor productivity.

Private Expenditures on Education

The gains in education attainment in the region may also be caused by increases in private spending. Not enough direct information is available on levels or trends in private expenditures to render a decisive judgment on this point. However, information on private enrollments provides indirect support for the view that private expenditures have taken up some of the slack created by falling public spending on education during the 1990s. Table 3.5 shows that the share of private enrollments has risen in most Middle Eastern and North African countries since 1985.

TABLE 3.5

Share of Private School Enrollments by Level of Education

(Percent)

Country	Primary				Secondary			
	1985	1990	1995	2000	1985	1990	1995	2000
Arab Republic of Egypt	4.8	5.76	6.5	8.06	—	—	4.8	6
Islamic Republic of Iran	—	0.14	—	3.56	—	0.3	—	5
Jordan	—	22.85	24.8	29.43	—	6.13	9.4	16
Lebanon	—	—	70.7	63.63	—	—	60.5	51.06
Morocco	3.4	3.59	3.8	4.62	6.3	2.66	2.7	5
Syria	4.5	3.55	3.9	4.33	6.2	5.58	5.9	4.8
Tunisia	0.4	0.54	0.6	0.77	9.5	11.99	8.6	7.64

Source: World Bank EdStats, www.worldbank.org/education/edstats.

Note: — Not available.

Education Quality Considerations

We have suggested that the significant gains in quantitative education attainments in the region during the last two decades may reflect increases in the efficiency of spending. This could have been brought about by specific measures to target underserved populations, reduce wasteful expenditures, and improve management. Box 3.1 provides an example of a program in Egypt that had these objectives and that has been working successfully since it was launched in 1996.

BOX 3.1

The Education Enhancement Program in Egypt

The Education Enhancement Program (EEP) was launched by the government of Egypt in 1996. The program has three main objectives: (a) increasing access to basic education, particularly for girls; (b) improving the quality of education; and (c) enhancing the efficiency of the education system in Egypt.

The first goal was approached through programs that involved building schools in poor and remote areas, especially those where female enrollment was unusually low, and attempting to increase parental demand for girls' education, through community awareness campaigns and a stipend program for qualifying families. The evidence to date suggests that this program is succeeding in raising girls' enrollment in targeted areas and in narrowing regional and gender disparities. Three results are notable. First, gross enrollment rates for girls have increased at a faster rate than the average. For example, although overall rates increased from 97.5 percent in 1995/96 to 105.8 percent in 2002/03, rates for girls increased from 93.4 percent to 103.2 percent. Second, some of the most dramatic increases have occurred in the poorer governorates of Upper Egypt. For example, between 1996/97 and 2002/03, girls' gross enrollment rose by 21 and 19 percentage points, respectively, in Beni Suef and Fayoum, two of the poorest governorates in Egypt. Third, analysis shows that the increases are statistically attributable to EEP efforts: girls' enrollment rates rose in direct proportion to the amount of new schools built, and they rose faster in program areas where awareness-raising campaigns were conducted than in nonprogram areas.

The objective of improving schooling quality has been approached through programs to reduce overcrowding in classes and multishift teaching; to offer learning-support teachers to children with learning difficulties; to improve the quality of teachers through more pre-service and in-service training, especially in the use of technology; and to reform the educational inspection system to emphasise evaluation processes. Preliminary evidence suggests that dropout rates and grade repetition rates may be falling in targeted areas. However, a thorough evaluation of the quality-improvement objective of the EEP remains to be done.

(Box continues on the following page.)

BOX 3.1 (CONTINUED)

The third objective, that of enhancing the efficiency of the education system, has been approached through programs focused on strategic planning and management, information systems, motivation and accountability, and stakeholder capacity building and involvement.

Factors that have contributed to the success of the EEP to date include (a) the political commitment of the Egyptian government, reflected in adequate budget allocations to education; (b) institutional innovation, involving a break with traditional planning approaches in favor of using data and community participation to target new school location and undertake awareness campaigns; (c) a focus on specific issues that research and experience show matter more for girls than for boys, such as improving physical facilities and in-service teacher training; and (d) good coordination among government, community, and donor efforts to provide the institutional, financial, and operational resources required for the job.

Source: Iqbal and Riad, 2004.

However, it is also possible that some of the gains in quantity may have come at the expense of quality. It is possible that lower spending has resulted in a higher number of students per classroom, a higher ratio of pupils to teachers, and lower pay for teachers—all factors that could lead to lower-quality education being provided. We attempt to determine whether this has indeed been the case by looking at trends in pupil–teacher ratios and student repetition rates. Table 3.6 shows that pupil–teacher ratios have declined in the Middle East and North Africa since 1985 for both primary and secondary education, although not in a uniform manner. The same is true for pupil–teacher ratios among lower-middle-income countries. Repetition rates at the primary level have also declined, and here the trend is more uniform for the Middle East and North Africa. Thus, the argument that quality has declined cannot be sustained on the basis of the available data.

Nor is the region performing below par with respect to more directly observable measures of quality. Data collected under the Trends in International Mathematics and Science Study allow an assessment of comparative education quality in mathematics and sciences for several countries in the region. Table 3.7 shows average scores achieved by eighth-graders in mathematics in 2003. Although the scores are low in absolute terms, they are about what might be expected on an income-adjusted basis for most Middle Eastern and North African countries (Carnoy 2005).

Nevertheless, complacency is not warranted. The educational challenges of the future are going to be different from those of the past. Until recently, providing access to education for a wide group of citizens

TABLE 3.6

Trends in Pupil–Teacher Ratios and Repetition Rates

Country Group	Education Quality Indicator	1985	1990	1995	2000
Lower-middle income	Pupil–teacher ratio, primary	26.02	23.07	24.04	21.65
Middle East and North Africa	Pupil–teacher ratio, primary	26.14	23.38	24.54	23.64
Lower-middle income	Pupil–teacher ratio, secondary	18.54	16.68	16.61	—
Middle East and North Africa	Pupil–teacher ratio, secondary	19.8	20.05	17.19	—
Lower-middle income	Repetition rate (%), primary	—	6.59	3.1	4.73
Middle East and North Africa	Repetition rate (%), primary	10.16	9.8	8.2	7.83

Source: World Bank EdStats, www.worldbank.org/education/edstats.

Note: — Not available.

TABLE 3.7

2003 Trends in International Mathematics and Science Study Math Scores

Country	Score
Malaysia	508
Bulgaria	476
Romania	475
Cyprus	459
Lebanon	433
Jordan	424
Islamic Republic of Iran	411
Indonesia	411
Tunisia	410
Arab Republic of Egypt	406
Chile	387
Morocco	387
Philippines	378

Source: Trends in International Mathematics and Science Study, accessible at http://nces.ed.gov/timss/.

was an important challenge and one met successfully in many of the region's countries. In the future it will be necessary to ensure that education serves the needs of entrepreneurs and workers who face greater competition both domestically and abroad. Much greater attention will have to be paid to the quality of education and its relevance to the labor market. In this regard, the level of information and communication technology connectivity may be relevant to the region's preparedness for the future. A recent United Nations Development Programme report noted that Arab countries rank very low in terms of such proxies for access to knowledge as the number of Internet hosts per 1,000 people. Indeed, in relative terms Arab countries are found to have a lower level of access on average than all other regions of the world, including regions with much lower incomes (UNDP 2002, figure 2.9). This may reflect deficiencies in the science and technology curricula of the Middle Eastern and North African Region's educational systems as well as government policies with respect to facilitating information sharing within and across borders.

Note

1. These are officially reported levels of unemployment. Underemployment is widely thought to be an even more serious problem in the region.

CHAPTER 4

Health and Poverty

As shown in chapter 2, the Middle East and North Africa Region has made significant progress in improving the average health status of its citizens. During the last two decades, the rate of progress has been above and beyond what can be explained by its initial levels of income and health in 1980 and subsequent income growth. This chapter explores patterns of health spending that may have contributed to this and discusses the extent to which improvements have occurred in the health status of the poor specifically. Key conclusions are (a) despite substantial gains, health disparities continue to exist between the poor and the rich, albeit to different extents in different countries; (b) health spending and outcomes vary among Middle Eastern and North African countries, reflecting different degrees of system efficiency; and (c) coping with the disease patterns emerging from the ongoing demographic transition will require new approaches to health care financing that should aim *inter alia* at protecting budget resources to address the needs of the poor.

Health and Poverty: The Record in the Middle East and North Africa

Figure 4.1 shows how health status has improved in most of the region during the past 40 years, according to the measure of child mortality. There is steady improvement in the case of each of the 10 countries shown here. And the same general picture of improvement applies in the case of other commonly used indicators of health, such as life expectancy or infant mortality. The question that arises is whether the gains in average health status have also redounded to the benefit of the poor. We investigate this first by looking at the disparities in health status that exist across income groups in the region, and then by checking to see if these disparities have been reduced over time.

FIGURE 4.1

Country-Specific Trends in Mortality among Children Less than 5 Years of Age, 1960–2000

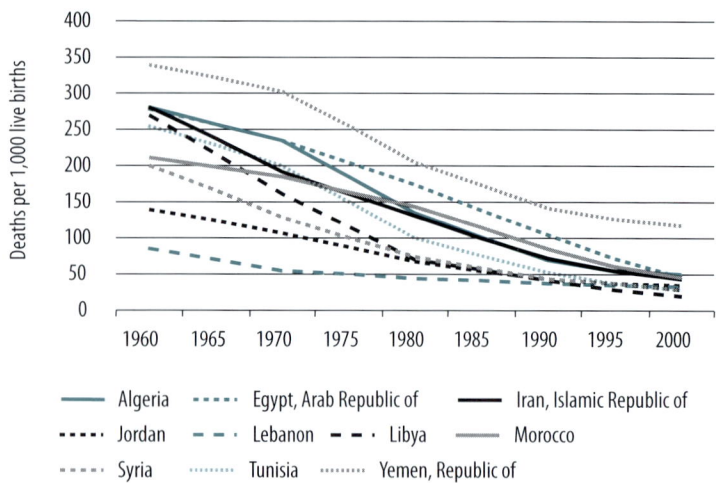

Source: World Development Indicators, CD-ROM 2004.

Health and wealth are frequently correlated. A sense of the extent of the correlation in this region can be obtained from recent Demographic and Health Survey (DHS) data for Egypt, Jordan, Morocco, and the Republic of Yemen.[1] These data show that for all four countries and for all five indicators (see figure 4.2), health outcomes among the poorest are worse than among the richest. On average across the four countries, the children of the poorest 20 percent of the population are more than twice as likely to die before they reach their fifth birthday, compared with the children of the richest group. More than four times as many mothers in the poorest group are malnourished, compared with mothers in the richest group. Children in the poorest segment of the population also have rates of malnutrition that are four times as high as those in the richest segment.

The extent of health inequalities varies among these four countries, with Egypt and Morocco having the largest disparities. In these two countries, under-five mortality rates are three times as high for the poorest quintile as for the richest, and infant mortality rates are more than twice as high. Among the poorest quintiles in Egypt and Morocco, infant mortality rates are over 75 per 1,000 live births and under-five mortality rates are close to 100 per 1,000. This is worse than the average for South Asia. The Republic of Yemen also has substantial health inequalities. The poorest 20 percent of that country's population have among the highest infant and child mortality rates in the world, with rates similar to those

FIGURE 4.2

Health Outcome Inequalities in Selected Countries

(Ratio of data for the poorest quintile to the richest quintile)

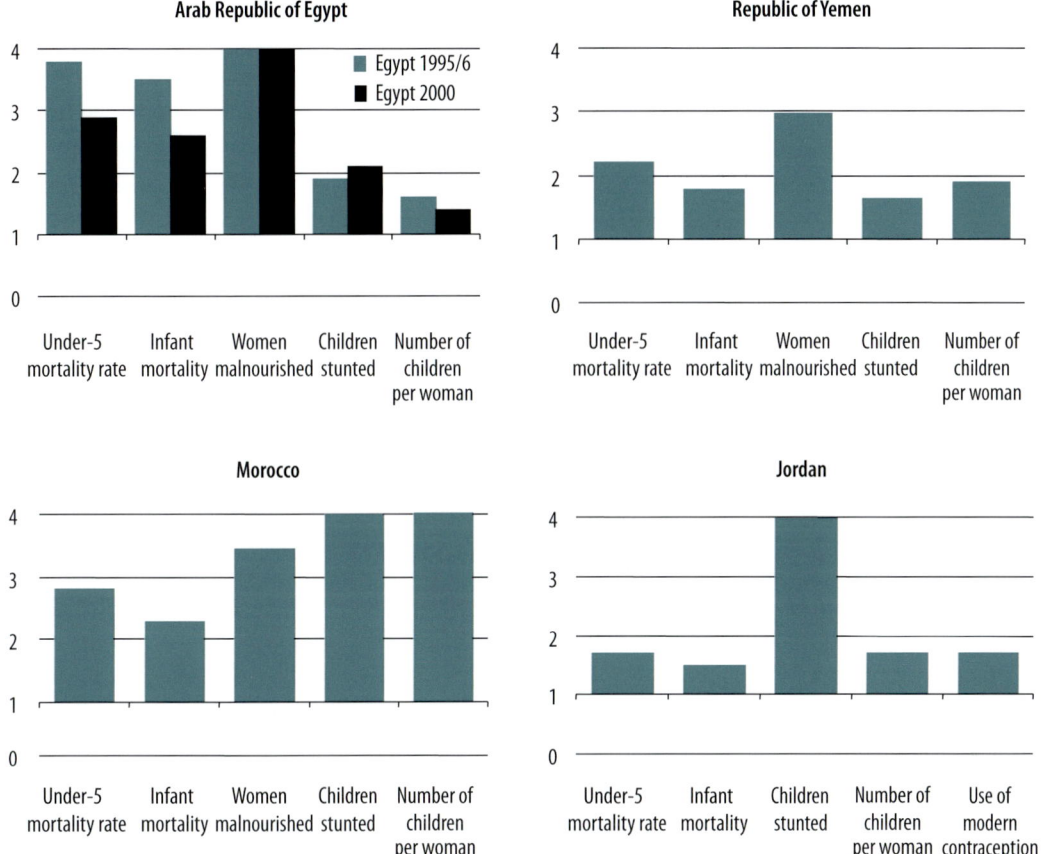

Sources: Demographic and Health Surveys for the Arab Republic of Egypt (1995/96, 2000), Jordan (1997), Morocco (1992), and the Republic of Yemen (1997).

found among the poorest people in Sub-Saharan Africa and South Asia. Jordan has much less health inequality than the other three countries. Indeed, it is among the lowest third in terms of health inequality among all countries covered by the DHS studies. Despite this, differences between the richest and the poorest Jordanians are still significant for child malnutrition and certain health process indicators.

Significant disparities at a given point in time, however, can still be consistent with a record of reduction of disparities over time. In general, the substantial decline of child and infant mortality in the region over the past four decades must reflect disproportionately higher health gains among the poor, compared with the rich. But it is useful to get more direct evidence as well. This is possible for the case of Egypt because two

DHSs have been completed there, one in 1995 and the other in 2000. Comparing across these two surveys shows that disparities have declined in Egypt for four of the five measures of health status (see figure 4.2, first panel). For other countries, indirect evidence may be used. For example, during the last two decades or so, the gap in infant mortality rates between rural and urban areas in the Islamic Republic of Iran has declined significantly. This suggests that the general improvement in health status there (as shown, for example, in figure 4.1) has been accompanied by disproportionate improvements in the health status of that republic's poor people. Box 4.1 discusses the factors that lie behind the Islamic Republic of Iran's impressive achievements in primary health care.

While acknowledging the improvements that have occurred to date, it is necessary to draw attention once again to the health inequality challenges that remain. Health policy in the region must continue to pay at-

---

BOX 4.1

Primary Health Care and the Rural Poor in the Islamic Republic of Iran

Rural households in the Islamic Republic of Iran traditionally have been the most disadvantaged segment of Iranian society, not only in terms of income and political power but also in accessing basic public services, including health. A major achievement of public policy in the Islamic Republic of Iran over the past 20 years has been the improvement of rural health and the near-elimination of some health disparities between urban and rural populations, the latter often comprising a much poorer group than the former. For example, in 1974 the infant mortality rate was 120 and 62 per thousand live births for rural and urban areas, respectively. By 2000, however, both the level and the differential of infant mortality had declined considerably—to 30 for rural areas and 28 for urban ones. This reduction in the rural–urban infant mortality gap was achieved in large measure through three innovations in the primary health care (PHC) system: (a) establishing "health houses" in remote and sparsely populated villages; (b) staffing the health houses with health workers, known as *behvarzan*, recruited from local communities; and (c) developing a simple but well-integrated health information system.

The health house, usually the only health facility accessible to the rural population, is the most basic unit of the Iranian PHC network. Located in individual villages, it is designed to cover a target population of about 1,500; each health house also serves several satellite villages selected with careful attention to their cultural and social compatibility. The distance between the village in which the health house is located and the satellite villages it serves is typically no more than one hour's walk. Tasks performed at the health house include record-keeping and data collection; public health education and promotion of community participation; antenatal, perinatal, and postnatal care; care of small children as well as school-age children; family planning services; immunization; and disease control services.

tention to reducing the large disparities that remain between rich and poor people through such measures as extending health insurance coverage to the poor, allocating more health resources (such as doctors, nurses, and clinics) to rural or otherwise poor areas, and implementing multifaceted community-level interventions to reach the poor.

Determinants of Health Achievements in the Middle East and North Africa

The pattern of health status improvement shown by countries in the region is also exhibited by most other developing regions. Indeed, there has been a global wave of improvement during the past four or five decades in such indicators as life expectancy and infant and child mortality. This global

Behvarzan who staff the health houses are chosen from among local people familiar with the households in the village. This facilitates the accurate collection of health information as well as culture-sensitive communication. Potential *behvarzan* receive free training and financial support throughout the two-year period of their training. In return, they are formally obliged to remain and serve at the village health house for a minimum of four years after completing their training.

The health information system enables the *behvarzan* to collect detailed data on rural communities. The main components of this information system are the household file (containing demographic and health information), various logbooks in which daily activities are recorded, and monthly report forms.

The PHC system is entirely funded by the national government, and the pattern of public health spending is oriented toward rural public health services—a fact that may partly explain its good performance with respect to rural infant mortality rates. Among specific measures taken by the PHC system are the promotion of healthy attitudes and behaviors; the universal immunization of children; and encouragement of mothers to breastfeed, use iodated salt, and provide appropriate treatment for children suffering from diarrhea and acute respiratory infections.

The presence of the community-friendly *behvarzan* in the village, with their constant interaction with the community, has helped ensure that health messages have not gone unheeded. Moreover, the ability of the PHC system to support the health messages by providing easy access to the means needed (vaccines, oral rehydration therapy, essential drugs, and so on) where and when they are required has also helped in bridging the gaps often found among knowledge, attitudes, and practice.

Source: Mehryar 2004.

trend is attributable to (a) improvements in medical science and technology and (b) improvements in public health interventions, including cost-effective programs of immunization. However, as shown in chapter 2, health status improvements in the Middle East and North Africa have been faster than in comparable countries. Indeed, for measures of child mortality and life expectancy the gaps that existed in earlier decades between countries in this region and comparator nations were eliminated by 2000. This suggests that there are factors beyond the common global wave of technological improvement that have influenced health achievements in this region. One such factor is likely to have been increases in female education. This is an area in which the Middle East and North Africa has made rapid improvements, although it has not yet closed the gap with comparators. Among other likely factors are levels and patterns of spending on health.

Levels of Spending on Health

Have Middle Eastern and North African countries tended to spend more on health than have comparable countries? Unfortunately, an extensive time series on health sector spending is not available so we cannot arrive at a definitive answer to this question. The available data do show somewhat higher spending in this region in recent years. Data for 2002 (see table 4.1) show that, on average, Middle Eastern and North African countries spend around 5.9 percent of GDP on health, which is just above the 5.8 percent spent by other lower-middle-income countries. However, the public spending component of this is 2.9 percent in the Middle East and North Africa, compared with 2.5 percent in other lower-middle-income countries. And per capita expenditures in the region are around $89, whereas those in lower-middle-income countries are around $75. There is a lot of variation within the region with regard to health spending, however, so the averages need to be interpreted with caution. Moreover, the variation in spending is not necessarily associated with differences in health outcomes (see box 4.2).

Incidence of Health Spending

We turn now to some evidence on patterns of spending. The limited amount of information on the incidence of health subsidies by income group in the region shows that the rich capture a larger fraction of the subsidies available through public spending on health. For example, in Algeria the share of household health expenditure for the poorest 10 percent of the urban population is three times higher than the share for the richest 10 percent; for the rural population it is twice as large (World Bank 1999b). In the Republic of Yemen, an analysis of the public health

TABLE 4.1

Health Expenditures in 2002

Country	Health Expenditure (% of GDP)			Health Expenditure (US$ per capita)
	Public	Private	Total	
Algeria	3.2	1.1	4.3	77
Arab Republic of Egypt	2.4	3.6	6.0	79
Islamic Republic of Iran	2.9	3.1	6.0	104
Jordan	4.3	5.0	9.3	165
Lebanon	3.5	8.0	11.5	568
Morocco	1.5	3.1	4.6	55
Syria	2.3	2.8	5.1	58
Tunisia	2.8	2.8	5.6	126
Republic of Yemen	1.0	2.7	3.7	23
Middle East and North Africa	2.9	3.0	5.9	89
Lower-middle-income countries	2.5	3.3	5.8	75

Source: World Development Indicators, CD-ROM 2004.

BOX 4.2

Health Expenditures and Outcomes in Selected Middle Eastern and North African Countries

Moderate Spending with Good Value for the Money: Tunisia

Health expenditure per capita in Tunisia is US$126 a year, out of which 50 percent derives from public sources. Health expenditures make up 5.6 percent of GDP. The level of health expenditure is comparable with international data for countries at similar income levels, although Tunisia is performing better than expected on key health outcomes, including life expectancy at birth, infant and child mortality rates, and maternal mortality rates. The state provides free or subsidized health care to the lowest income groups, and the level of health coverage to the Tunisian population is high compared with many other middle-income countries.

High Private Spending and Limited Access for Poor People: Lebanon

As a share of national income, Lebanon and Jordan spend a larger proportion on health than many Organisation for Economic Co-operation and Development countries (11.5 and 9.3 percent, respectively). With US$568 in per capita health expenditures a year, Lebanon is by far the highest spender on health in the Middle East and North Africa. Unique for the region, the private sector dominates health financing and service provision in Lebanon. A large share of health expenditure is taken up by costly tertiary care and pharmaceuticals for the well-off population, and most poor people do not have access to care. Lebanon is considered an underperformer with respect to health outcomes (as measured by child mortality and life expectancy).

(Box continues on the following page.)

BOX 4.2 (CONTINUED)

High Public Spending and Good Access for Poor People: Jordan
Jordan has the highest share of public spending on health to GDP among the countries in the Middle East and North Africa for which data are available, and it possesses a health system that provides good access to the poor. Despite the universal public health coverage in Jordan, there is some regressivity in health financing, with the poorest quintile paying proportionally slightly more out of pocket for outpatient care (9 percent of household income), compared with the out-of-pocket expenditures of the richest quintile (7 percent). The high level of health expenditure, at US$165 per person a year, raises concerns about financial sustainability. There are structural inefficiencies that will have to be addressed in light of the epidemiologic and demographic transition that will increase both demand for and cost of services.

Low Spending and Limited Access for Poor People: Republic of Yemen
The Republic of Yemen spends only US$23 on health per capita a year. This is below the World Health Organization's recommended US$30–40 per person annually to cover basic health care costs, although it is above the minimum annual US$12 per person estimated for preventive and essential clinical services. Although total health spending increased from 2.5 percent of GDP in 1994 to about 3.7 percent in 2002, it is still among the lowest in the region, and is low compared with other low-income countries that average around 5 percent. The mix between public and private spending is tilted toward the latter, and out-of-pocket health spending as a share of national income in the Republic of Yemen is the second-highest in the Middle East and North Africa (after Lebanon). Nevertheless, results to date have been encouraging. When its endowments (of income and social indicators) and spending are controlled for, the Republic of Yemen has been among the stronger performers in the region in improving child mortality and life expectancy.

subsidies provided through health facilities found the subsidies to be mildly progressive in that the subsidy as a percentage of household per capita expenditure tends to be higher for the poor. However, absolute subsidy levels were almost twice as high for the richest quintile as for the poorest, and households in the richest quintile receive 26 percent of public health expenditure compared with 16 percent for the poorest. The nonpoor population spends about 10 percent of its total health expenditure for treatment outside the country (World Bank 2002f). In the Islamic Republic of Iran, pharmaceuticals are heavily subsidized, with a cost to the government equal to 0.8 percent of GDP in 1998. Although the share in *total* consumption of pharmaceuticals is higher for the poor than for the nonpoor, the *absolute* consumption among the nonpoor is much higher than among the poor. The richest people accordingly receive by far the larger share of the benefits from the pharmaceutical subsidy.

Pattern of Spending

Private spending on health accounts for about half of all health spending in the region, and insurance makes up only a small fraction of this. In other words, most private spending represents out-of-pocket outlays. The significant reliance on out-of-pocket spending means that many households have little or no financial protection in the event of a catastrophic illness or injury. Such vulnerability is higher among lower-income households. In general, such households allocate higher proportions of their budgets to health care services. For example, in the Republic of Yemen the rural and poorer population spends a higher share of household expenditures on health care services than do urban inhabitants. Health expenditures represent 1.3–2.0 percent of household expenditures for the poorest quintile in rural areas, compared with 0.6–1.6 percent for the poorest quintile in urban regions. The design of sustainable health insurance schemes to mitigate such risks among the poor and the near-poor should be considered a matter of high priority in the region.

Health Challenges Arising from Demographic and Epidemiologic Transition

Health challenges of the future are likely to be different from those in the past, in part because of the ongoing demographic and epidemiologic transition. In the 1980s and early 1990s the Middle East and North Africa had the highest population growth rate of any region in the world. Population growth slowed in most countries in the 1990s and is now about 2 percent for the region as a whole (which is still higher than all regions except Sub-Saharan Africa). It is estimated that by 2015 the number of adults in the region will have increased by 140 percent, representing the highest adult population growth in the world after Sub-Saharan Africa.

Over the next two decades, health patterns in the Middle East and North Africa will be profoundly influenced by continued declines in fertility and mortality as countries go through the demographic transition. A further 50 percent decline in fertility with modest gains in life expectancy is projected for the region by the World Bank. The overall effect of the declines in fertility and mortality is a dramatic shift in the age structure and causes of morbidity and mortality (WBI 2004; World Bank 2002c). Several countries in the region will soon have 5 percent or more of their populations over age 65. Some of the lower-middle-income countries in the region, including Lebanon, the Islamic Republic of Iran, and Tunisia, are well advanced in the demographic transition, with low birth rates (around two children per woman) and low mortality. Algeria, Egypt,

FIGURE 4.3

Trends in Deaths, by Cause, in the MENA Region
(Percent)

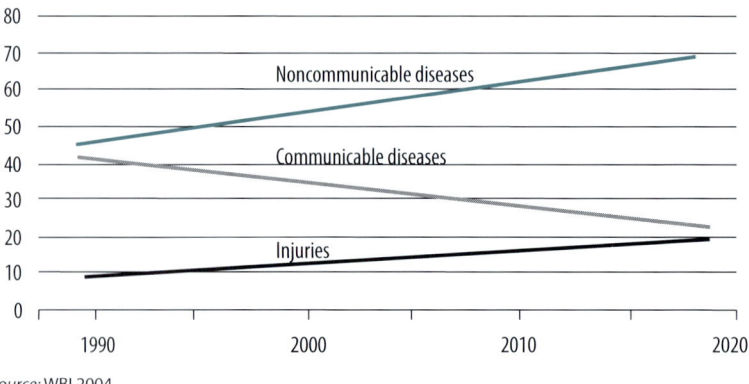

Source: WBI 2004.

Jordan, Morocco, and Syria are in mid-transition, with declining fertility and low mortality rates.

The challenges of an aging population include a substantial rise in noncommunicable diseases and increasing demand for costly long-term care (see figure 4.3). In addition to the impact of the demographic transition, rapid urbanization and changing lifestyles have contributed to an increase in noncommunicable diseases and injuries in the region. Dealing with these challenges may have implications for the poor. The emerging disease patterns require individual-oriented and technology-intensive treatment regimes that are expensive. Thus an increasing share of health budget resources is likely to be pulled toward the treatment of such cases. This may put the poor at a disadvantage if the needed resources are taken from services that address their needs. Indeed, there is some evidence that such a shift in resources already is occurring. In recent years, governments in the region have been investing in expensive medical technology to cope with the rising demand from urban middle-class populations. Finding a balance between competing demands to address the demographic and epidemiologic transition and improve access to quality health services for poor people represents a major challenge for the countries in the Middle East and North Africa.

Note

1. DHSs have been completed for 56 developing countries in recent years including four in the Middle East and North Africa—Egypt (1995 and 2000), Jordan (1997), Morocco (1992), and the Republic of Yemen (1997). These surveys provide information on selected health indicators disaggregated by income quintiles.

CHAPTER 5

Safety Nets and the Poor

Over the years most countries in the Middle East and North Africa Region have established extensive social protection programs to aid vulnerable groups in society (see table 5.1). Five program areas are briefly reviewed here: food subsidies, energy subsidies, cash transfers, public works, and microfinance.[1] The objective in each case is to assess the extent to which the region's poor people are helped through these programs and, wherever possible, to see whether program effectiveness has improved over time. For the most part, program details are provided in boxes or otherwise summarized.

There are five main findings. First, food subsidies are a prominent mechanism for helping the poor and protecting their purchasing power and nutritional status. Although outlays on food subsidies (as a proportion of GDP) have declined over time in most countries, their targeting has improved and they have become more pro-poor in their incidence. Second, energy subsidies are sizable in many countries (such as Egypt, the Islamic Republic of Iran, and the Republic of Yemen) but are not pro-poor in their distributional impact, and they represent a large untapped

TABLE 5.1

Spending on Selected Social Safety Net Programs, Late 1990s

(Percent of GDP)

Country	Food Subsidies	Cash Transfers	Public Works	Energy Subsidies
Algeria	0.0	0.4	0.2	—
Arab Republic of Egypt	1.7	0.2	0.3	4.6
Islamic Republic of Iran	2.7	1.2	—	10.0
Jordan	0.3	0.9	—	—
Morocco	1.7	0.1	0.2	2.0
Tunisia	1.2	0.5	0.1	—
Republic of Yemen	0.3	1.0	0.2	6.5

Sources: World Bank 2002d and staff estimates.

Note: — Not available. Energy subsidy estimates are for 2000–04 period.

source of funding that could be applied more efficiently to other social programs. Third, the cash transfer programs that exist are relatively better targeted to poor populations than are food and energy subsidies, but they are too small in scale to be effective poverty-fighting instruments. Fourth, many employment- and income-generating programs exist but it is hard to assess their impact. One rigorous assessment exercise carried out for Morocco shows substantial differences in poverty outcomes across programs, suggesting that specifics of design have an important influence on poverty impact. Fifth, microfinance programs have grown in size and reach during the last 10 years and they exhibit increasing pro-poor characteristics.

Food Subsidies

Food subsidies have existed in various Middle Eastern and North African countries for several decades and are an important element of the social protection system where they exist.[2] In most countries they take the form of broad-based universal subsidies and quantity rationing through ration cards. Typically they include wheat and wheat flour (or semolina in Tunisia), edible oil, and sugar. In most countries, food subsidies are provided as a direct price reduction to consumers. In some countries, such as Morocco, wheat flour prices are kept low through subsidies provided to millers. A brief description of food subsidy schemes in countries of the region is presented in box 5.1, and their costs are identified in table 5.2. As can be seen, *public spending on food subsidies declined in most Middle Eastern and North African countries during the 1990s*. This resulted from a variety of reform measures undertaken during this period. For example, in Egypt and Tunisia, measures were undertaken to improve the targeting of food subsidies to the poor, thereby reducing overall outlays during most of the 1990s. In Algeria, Jordan, and the Republic of Yemen, food subsidies were eliminated for the most part and replaced by cash transfers at different times during the 1990s.

Distributional Impact

Food subsidy programs in the region have tended to share three characteristics: they have been regressive in absolute terms, progressive in relative terms, and an important source of nutritional intake for the poor. Table 5.3 presents illustrative data for selected countries for various points in time during the 1990s. Regarding the first point, food subsidies are typically regressive in absolute terms because the nonpoor population consumes higher quantities of subsidized goods than do poor people. As

BOX 5. 1

Consumer Food Subsidy Programs in the Middle East and North Africa

Algeria: Between 1973 and 1996, consumer food subsidies grew to cover a wide range of items, including bread, milk, sugar, cooking oil, and other items. Subsidies were both explicit, through a government transfer, and implicit, through exchange rate overvaluation and fixed prices and margins. Until 1982 explicit subsidies were funded entirely though budget support. When this proved unsustainable, subsidies were financed through an extrabudgetary account, *Fonds de Compensation*. Although beneficial for the poor, the system was inefficient and costly, reaching almost 5 percent of GDP. In 1992, in the context of a broader structural adjustment program, the Algerian government began to gradually reduce the subsidies on some food items. By the end of the 1990s most food subsidies had been eliminated (World Bank 1999a).

Egypt: By the late 1970s the subsidy system covered almost 20 food items and absorbed about 20 percent of total government spending. Fueled by rapid population growth and a depreciating currency, the system became fiscally unsustainable. Initial attempts to raise prices on subsidized goods were met with riots, and the price hikes were rescinded. The authorities then adopted a gradual approach under which (a) the number of subsidized commodities was reduced to only four—*baladi* bread, coarse flour, edible oil, and sugar; (b) the number of ration card holders was reduced by introducing a two-tier system of full subsidy (green books) and partial subsidy (red books); and (c) prices of key foods, especially bread and sugar, were allowed to rise (Adams 2000). This pattern of adjustment was partially reversed in 2004 when new items were added to the ration card system to offset the rise in food prices brought about by the substantial exchange rate depreciation in 2003.

Jordan: Prior to 1991 universal subsidies were available on a number of commodities, including bread, flour, rice, sugar, and milk. The 1988 devaluation of the Jordanian dinar (JD) substantially increased the fiscal costs of the system, and in 1991 rationing was introduced for subsidized sugar, rice, and powdered milk. In 1994 an income-based criterion was adopted for the allocation of ration coupons. Only two-thirds of the population elected to obtain the coupons, thereby helping improve targeting and reduce costs. In 1996 the subsidies on bread and flour were eliminated (general wheat subsidies were replaced with targeted means-tested cash transfers), and in 1997 the equivalent cash transfer was merged with the existing scheme on rice and sugar. In 1999 the cash transfer scheme was phased out and replaced by targeted cash assistance through the National Aid Fund (NAF) (Shaban, Abu-Ghaida, and Al-Naimat 2001).

(Box continues on the following page.)

BOX 5.1 (CONTINUED)

Morocco: Currently two subsidized commodities are available to all: sugar and low-grade flour. The combination of quotas and price controls on certain subsidized commodities has led to considerable leakage and skimming by producers. Food subsidies in Morocco generally tend to compensate consumers for the incidence of high border tariffs and to protect crop producers and industrial processors (World Bank 1999).

Islamic Republic of Iran: Subsidies are provided on a range of foodstuffs, including flour, pasteurized milk, sugar, vegetable oil, meat, chicken, and eggs. In recent years the subsidy program has been financed almost exclusively through direct budgetary allocations, whereas until the late 1990s some implicit subsidization occurred through an overvalued exchange rate as well. By 1996 the system absorbed more than 11 percent of total government spending and 2.7 percent of GDP. At various points in the 1990s, reforms were attempted through such measures as reducing a number of commodities in the coupon system; introducing cash transfers to replace coupons on eggs and chicken; and raising controlled prices on meat and sugar (World Bank 1999a).

Tunisia: Food subsidies are administered through the *Caisse Generale de Compensation*. Up to 1990 the subsidy scheme covered cereals (durum wheat and bread wheat), edible oils, milk, and sugar in unlimited amounts available to all citizens. This approach made subsidies cheap to administer but poorly targeted and fiscally expensive. Starting in 1990 the government improved the targeting efficiency of the subsidy scheme by introducing self-selection mechanisms through quality differentiation of subsidized goods. Subsidies on key products consumed predominantly by the poor were maintained while those consumed by the nonpoor were reduced or eliminated (World Bank 1996).

TABLE 5.2

Food Subsidy Costs, Selected Years, 1989–99

(Percent of GDP)

Country	1989	1992	1995	1999
Algeria	2.9	3.3	0.9	0.0
Arab Republic of Egypt	3.7	5.1	1.3	*1.7*
Islamic Republic of Iran	—	1.5	2.9	2.7
Jordan	3.1	1.5	1.4	0.3
Morocco	—	1.3	1.7	1.7
Tunisia	2.8	1.9	2.1	1.2
Republic of Yemen	—	3.7	2.6	0.3

Source: World Bank 2002d.

Note: — Not available. Data in italics are for closest year.

shown in table 5.3, with the exception of urban Egypt where the distribution is progressive, transfers to the richest quintile exceed those to the
poorest quintile. Leakage was particularly serious in the Republic of
Yemen in 1992: benefits to the rich were almost sevenfold those to the
poor.[3] The second characteristic, progressivity in relative terms, arises because the poor spend a bigger proportion of their incomes on food and
thus subsidized products represent a larger relative share of their total
spending. For instance, in Egypt (in 1997) and Tunisia (in 1990), subsi-

TABLE 5.3

Incidence of Food Subsidy Programs

(Percent)

Country (Year)	Poor 1	2	3	4	Rich 5	Average	Ratio of 5:1	Ratio of 1:5
Algeria (1991)								
Absolute incidence	13.3	16.8	18.8	21.9	29.2	100	2.2	0.45
Relative incidence	24.4	18.2	1.8	2.0	1.9	2.1	0.07	12.8
Nutritional impact	—	—	—	—	—	—		
Algeria (1995)								
Absolute incidence	—	—	—	—	—	—		
Relative incidence	20.8	16.5	14.0	11.7	8.1	14.2	0.39	2.57
Nutritional impact	34.5	30.5	28.9	27.6	25.4	24.4	0.74	1.36
Egypt, Arab Rep. of, urban (1997)								
Absolute incidence	20.8	21.4	22.1	18.9	16.8	100.0	0.81	1.23
Relative incidence	8.7	6.2	4.8	3.1	1.4	3.1	0.16	6.11
Nutritional impact	43.5	40.4	36.4	30.0	24.6	33.8	0.56	1.77
Egypt, Arab Rep. of, rural (1997)								
Absolute incidence	19.5	18.9	19.5	21.0	21.0	100.0	1.08	0.92
Relative incidence	8.9	6.1	5.1	4.2	2.6	4.9	0.29	3.42
Nutritional impact	37.9	32.4	30.5	31.8	28.5	31.6	0.75	1.33
Morocco (1995)								
Absolute incidence	15.0	19.0	20.0	21.0	25.0	100	1.7	0.6
Relative incidence	4.0	3.0	2.4	1.7	0.9	1.7	0.2	4.4
Nutritional impact	12.9	10.9	10.8	10.0	9.7	10.6	0.8	1.3
Tunisia (1990)								
Absolute incidence	17.0	20.0	21.0	22.0	20.0	100	1.2	0.9
Relative incidence	8.7	6.2	4.8	3.5	1.4	3.5	0.2	5.4
Nutritional impact	59.8	63.2	60.4	59.3	49.9	58.5	0.8	1.02
Tunisia (1993)								
Absolute incidence	21	20	21	20	18	100	0.9	1.1
Relative incidence	7.8	4.5	3.4	2.4	1.1	2.6	0.1	7.2
Nutritional impact	54.2	45.3	44.3	40.9	32.8	43.5	0.6	1.6
Republic of Yemen (1992)								
Absolute incidence	6.7	11.0	15.4	21.5	45.4	100.0	6.78	0.15
Relative incidence	10.8	11.1	11.8	10.5	10.4	—	0.96	1.04
Nutritional impact	—	—	—	—	—			

Source: World Bank 1999a.

Note: — Not available. Absolute incidence is the share of benefits accruing to quintile; relative incidence is expenditure on subsidized goods as
a share of total expenditure; nutritional impact is calorie intake from subsidized food as a share of total calorie intake.

dized foods accounted for about 9 percent of spending by the poor, compared with about 2 percent for the rich. Similar patterns were observed for Algeria (1995) and Morocco (1995), with the former exhibiting the most progressive pattern. The Republic of Yemen seems to be somewhat of an exception in that all income groups appear to benefit equally in relative terms. Finally, with regard to nutritional impact, or calorie intake from subsidized food as a share of total calorie intake, each country in the table shows a progressive pattern. For some countries, subsidized food provides a fairly high share of calories for the poor—up to 45 percent in urban Egypt (1997) and 60 percent in Tunisia (1990).

Changes in Food Subsidy Programs over Time

Several countries, including Algeria, Egypt, Jordan, Tunisia, and the Republic of Yemen, have undertaken reforms at various points in the last two decades to reduce the fiscal burden of food subsidies. A variety of reform schemes have been experimented with, including reducing the number of commodities subject to subsidies, reducing the number of beneficiaries through the introduction of means-tested ration cards, changing the mix of products available, and replacing food subsidies with targeted cash transfers.[4] It is hard to provide an overview of the impact of these reforms on the poor because not enough analysis has been done. The two cases for which some intertemporal information is available, namely Algeria (1995 and 1991) and Tunisia (1993 and 1990), show mixed results. In the case of Algeria, reforms introduced in 1991 appear to have had an adverse effect. The ratio of relative incidence of food subsidies dropped from 12.8 in favor of the poor to 2.6 by 1995 (see table 5.3). In the case of Tunisia, however, reforms had a more positive impact. Between 1990 and 1993 all three measures of incidence improved in favor of the poor.

Success in Tunisia appears to have been related to the government's ability to engage in product and quality differentiation through which subsidies applying to certain "luxury" qualities of foods were cut and those applying to "inferior" qualities were maintained. Such differentiation then induced a form of self-targeting in that mostly the poor were attracted to the subsidized products while the nonpoor, although eligible, chose not to buy the subsidized items. For example, subsidies on goods that were consumed predominantly by the nonpoor, such as baguettes, were removed and those on products consumed predominantly by poor people, such as semolina, were maintained (Alderman and Lindert 1998). A similar form of self-targeting was tried in Egypt: subsidies on higher-quality *fino* and *shami* bread were removed in 1992 and 1996, respectively, while those on *baladi* (coarse flour) bread, which is consumed largely by the poor, were maintained (Adams 2000).

The success of the self-targeting approach also relied in part on making available "superior" alternatives that drew consumption by the non-poor away from the subsidized commodities. For instance, in Tunisia milk subsidies were shifted to reconstituted milk packaged in cheaper cartons that were less attractive to wealthier consumers; concurrently, fresh, locally produced, sterilized milk (luxury product) stored in bottles or tetrabrik cartons (designed for longer storage) was promoted and made available in the market. In Egypt the government allowed the free market to produce and sell the larger and higher-quality bread, which tended to attract the demand of wealthier households away from the lower-quality *baladi* bread consumed by the poor (Adams 2000).

Some other lessons also may be derived from the food subsidy reform experience to date in the region. For example, reforms were clearly constrained by administrative considerations. In Tunisia attempts to reform the generalized subsidy system through individual assessment and geographic targeting methods failed because of administration and implementation constraints. Moreover, without a clear distinction among neighborhoods, geographic targeting of transfers was not a feasible option (Alderman and Lindert 1998). In Egypt attempts to limit eligibility to ration books through the introduction of a two-tier system were modest, undermined by limited capacity to administer means-tested transfers (Adams 2000). Similarly, in the Republic of Yemen, where food subsidies have been replaced by cash transfers through the Social Welfare Fund, coverage is limited by weak administrative capacity compounded by complex and burdensome targeting procedures. Capacity constraints in the republic also have translated into higher administrative costs of delivering benefits. Administrative costs of the Social Welfare Fund are estimated at around 14 percent of total program costs, compared with an average of 4–6 percent for targeted programs (World Bank 2002f). In Jordan, by contrast, adequate institutional and administrative capacity have supported improved targeting of benefits while reducing overall costs (including administrative ones) and subsequently eliminating food subsidies.[5]

Energy Subsidies

In some Middle Eastern and North African countries energy subsidies are substantial. Calculations done at various points during the years 2000–04 suggest subsidy rates as high as 10 percent of GDP in the Islamic Republic of Iran, 6.5 percent of GDP in the Republic of Yemen, and 4.6 percent in Egypt. Since 2004, oil prices have risen substantially and the implied subsidies are likely to have grown. Who benefits from these subsidies?

Distributional incidence calculations suggest that energy subsidies benefit mostly the nonpoor population. In the Islamic Republic of Iran, spending on energy constitutes a greater proportion of total consumption by poor households compared with the consumption by nonpoor households, with the share being higher in rural areas mostly because of the higher consumption of kerosene. However, with consumption of the rich being much higher in absolute terms than that of the poor, a significant portion of the subsidy is essentially captured by those who are not poor (see figure 5.1). The leakage rate for energy subsidies (that is, the share of subsidy accruing to the nonpoor) is estimated at 94 percent in urban areas and 89 percent in rural areas (World Bank 2003a). For the Republic of Yemen two recent studies yield similar views on the distribution of energy subsidies. In one (van de Walle 2002), inferences are made on the basis of information on ownership of power generators and their use for lighting and irrigation purposes. These suggest that diesel and electricity subsidies largely benefit the rich, especially in rural areas, because the poor are likely to consume much smaller amounts than are richer households. A more recent study (World Bank 2004f) based on an Energy Sector Management Assistance Program survey reported that about 85 percent of the petroleum subsidy goes to the nonpoor, who consume seven times more diesel and 50 percent more liquefied petroleum gas (LPG) than do the poor. However, elimination of subsidies could have an adverse impact on poor people unless they are compensated in some other fashion. This is because petroleum subsi-

FIGURE 5.1

Incidence of Energy Subsidies in the Islamic Republic of Iran

(Rials per day, 2000 prices)

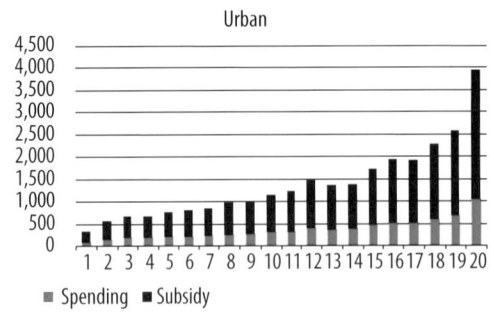
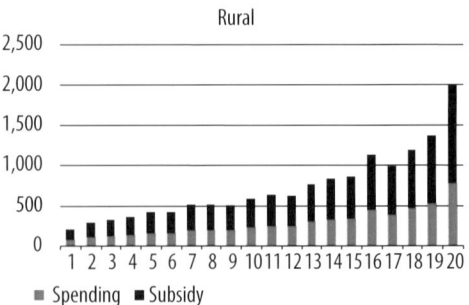

Source: World Bank 2003a.

dies do have a sizable impact on transportation costs and food prices and these items account for substantial shares in the expenditure patterns of the poor.

Similar distributional results were found in a recent analysis of energy subsidies in Egypt (World Bank 2005b). Rich households benefit much more from these subsidies than do poor households: whereas the top quintile receives 34 percent of benefits from subsidies on four petroleum products (LPG, gasoline, kerosene, and natural gas), the poorest quintile of the population receives only 13 percent. As in other countries, the regressive pattern is not uniform across different products. Gasoline tends to be the most regressive, with 93 percent of benefits going to the richest quintile, whereas kerosene tends to be the least. Indeed, in Egypt the kerosene subsidy is progressive in that the poorest quintile benefits more than does the richest quintile (see figure 5.2).

Given their size, the redesign of energy subsidies could release huge resources for spending on other parts of the social safety net. For example, a recent calculation for Egypt (World Bank 2005b) showed that if current non-kerosene energy subsidies were cut in half (to about 4.5 percent of GDP) and the saved revenues were distributed equally to the entire population of Egypt as a cash transfer, the incidence of poverty would be cut to 13.5 percent (from a level of around 20 percent). Some 4.2 million people would be lifted above the poverty line. It should go without saying that if targeted transfers were attempted, the reduction in poverty would be even more substantial.

FIGURE 5.2

Incidence of Petroleum Subsidies in the Arab Republic of Egypt, 2004

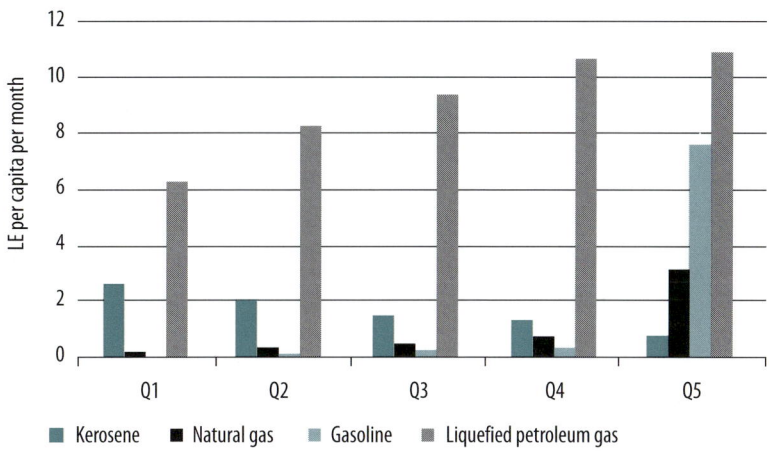

Source: World Bank 2005b.

Cash Assistance Programs

Several Middle Eastern and North African countries have some form of cash assistance program for the poor. Although the schemes vary in coverage and scope (see box 5.2), most are targeted not at the poor per se but at vulnerable groups such as widows, orphans, the disabled, the unemployed, and the elderly. *Two common features are low targeting efficiency and low ratios of transfers relative to the incomes of the poor.* For example, in Egypt only 14 percent of one popular cash transfer scheme (often called the *Sadat Pension*) is actually received by those defined as poor according to the national poverty line. This proportion goes up to 60 percent if the poor are defined as being the bottom 40 percent of the population. Furthermore, cash transfers amount to only 4 percent of poverty line income in the aggregate (data from 2000). In Jordan only 33 percent of such transfers reach those defined as highly vulnerable; however, average transfers for the poorest deciles are much higher than those for the richest deciles (data from 2002). In the Republic of Yemen the main cash transfer program, the Social Welfare Fund, covers less than 5 percent of the poor population (data from 1999) but, like Jordan, the mean per capita transfer is higher for the poor than for the nonpoor. Only in Tunisia is the situation much better. There, almost 72 percent of poor families are covered by cash transfer programs, and the transfer amounts are as high as 25 percent of the poverty line.

Public Works Programs

By providing employment during times of temporary distress, such as droughts, recessions, or slack agricultural seasons, public works programs can help mitigate the risks of various shocks on vulnerable groups, and provide poorer communities with basic physical infrastructure. The antipoverty impact of public works programs depends to a considerable extent on specific design features, including (a) the level of the wage rate, which ideally should be set slightly below the market wage to promote self-selection of the poor into the programs; (b) the labor intensity, which affects the volume of jobs created by the programs; and (c) the duration and timing of public works activity, to assess the risk-reducing or income-stabilizing effect of these programs (Subbarao 2003).[6]

An overview based on data for various years and various programs in four countries—Egypt, Morocco, Tunisia, and the Republic of Yemen—has provided evidence of great variety in program design, funding levels, and outputs. Taking funding levels and outputs first, the available evidence showed a range of annual spending from $16 million in Tunisia

BOX 5.2

Main Cash Transfer Programs in the Middle East and North Africa

Egypt: The Ministry of Social Affairs and Insurance (MOSAI) runs a special program, known as *ma'ash daman*, for the destitute and those who are not covered by any program of social insurance or security. This program is further subdivided into two main schemes: (a) guaranteed assistance (also known as pensions but different from conventional contribution-based pensions) and (b) non-guaranteed or temporary assistance awarded on a case-by-case basis to help poor individuals cope with unforeseen emergencies. The guaranteed programs account for about 90 percent of total payments whereas the temporary programs account for only about 10 percent. Beneficiaries include vulnerable groups such as the disabled, orphans, widows, divorced women and their children, and prisoners' families. In 2001–02, MOSAI distributed just over 500 million Egyptian pounds of cash assistance to approximately 900,000 families at the rate of about 560 Egyptian pounds (or roughly US$180 at the 2001–02 exchange rate) per recipient family per year.

Tunisia: The main form of social assistance to poor and needy families is provided by the Ministry of Social Affairs through the *Familles Necessiteuses* program. In 1994 the program covered about 107,000 families, of which 60 percent were in rural areas. The ministry further administers two direct transfer schemes: (a) food aid through school programs and food rations for preschoolers (about 300,000 children) and (b) social assistance to disabled people and the elderly poor population (about 10,000 people). Support to needy families also takes the form of occasional aid to cover such items as food, clothing, and drugs, provided during occasions such as religious festivities or return to school. Occasional and regular transfers, which were originally administered by the *Union Tunisienne de Solidarite Sociale*, are now managed within the broader *Programme National d'Aide aux Familles Necessiteuses* set up with the structural adjustment program in 1986.

Jordan: Cash benefits are administered through the National Aid Fund (NAF). Established in 1986 with the purpose of institutionalizing social security in Jordan, NAF's role was strengthened with the removal of the generalized food subsidy system in 1999, and the concurrent expansion of its cash assistance program to offset the welfare loss on poorer population groups. NAF's main social assistance scheme is the Income Supplement Program (accounted for 94 percent of NAF expenditure in 2002), and is targeted to vulnerable and chronically poor households, including orphans, divorced and abandoned women, elderly and physically disabled people, and prisoners' families. Other forms of assistance also include Cash Assistance for Handicapped Care and the Emergency and Exceptional Aid Programs (about 5 percent of NAF budget). Because of the relatively limited coverage of the Income Supplement Program (it covered only 30 percent of the poor), the system was expanded in 2002 to include not only the poor who cannot work but also the working poor. The new system was renamed the Family Income Supplement Program. In 2002 NAF's expenditure on all its programs amounted to

(Box continues on the following page.)

BOX 5.2 (CONTINUED)

0.61 percent of GDP—a modest amount compared with the housing subsidy (0.7 percent) or formal pensions to public servants (4.0 percent) (World Bank 2004d).

The Republic of Yemen: The Social Welfare Fund (SWF) is the government's primary targeted social assistance program. The SWF was established in 1996 to mitigate the adverse effect of subsidy removal on the poor. The program relies on a two-tier targeting system: a first stage of geographic targeting based on poverty incidence; and a second stage based on indicator (category) targeting, given the geographic allocation. Target groups include orphans, widows, divorced women, and people who are permanently disabled, poor, and elderly—eligible for permanent or guaranteed assistance if they do not receive income from other sources such as pensions or the Martyr's Fund. Temporary assistance is granted to the temporarily disabled and to prisoners' families, for which annual renewals cannot exceed three years. Under this program beneficiaries are eligible for a transfer of YR1,000 per month, with a YR200 supplement for each additional dependent up to a maximum of YR24,000 per year. For a family of six, this translates to YR333 per person per month or about 10 percent of the national poverty line in 1998 (van de Walle 2002).

(during 1987–91), to $25 million in Egypt (1997–2001), to $42 million in Morocco (between 1990 and 1999). Employment outcomes have varied as follows: 75,000 person-years in Tunisia, 43,000 in Egypt, and 40,000 in Morocco. These numbers yield rough estimates of cost per person-year of job created, ranging from a low of $213 for Tunisia, to $581 for Egypt, and to a high of $1,050 for Morocco. This wide range in costs per job suggests that consistency of definitions may be a problem; in other words, the definition of jobs and of costs may vary from country to country.

In terms of design, labor intensity is observed to vary significantly across countries and types of assets. In Morocco, labor content varied from 17 to 86 percent for rural roads projects, 31 to 47 percent for water projects, and 30 to 40 percent for social infrastructure projects. This is broadly consistent with international norms for labor content in infrastructure projects, where the cost of labor ranged from 40 to 50 percent of total cost for road construction projects, and from 70 to 80 percent for road or drainage maintenance projects, as well soil conservation and reforestation projects (Subbarao 2003). In Tunisia it is estimated that 80 percent of program costs go to unskilled workers, although no breakdown by type of project is available. This performance exceeds ratios realized for the Maharashtra Employment Guarantee scheme in India, where the wage bill constituted 70 percent of total cost (Subbarao 2003). In the Republic of Yemen, labor content is rather low, es-

timated at only 30 percent of project costs—10 percent of which is received by locally recruited unskilled labor, and 20 percent of which goes
to skilled labor contracted from outside communities. In Egypt no information on labor intensity of projects is available, and although projects are designed to ensure built-in labor-intensive techniques, there is
some evidence suggesting most program activities are capital intensive,
especially water and sewerage projects, with the wage share amounting
to only 30 percent of total costs as in the Republic of Yemen (World
Bank 2002d).

In terms of timing and duration of public works programs, there is evidence that these programs are scaled up during times of drought in Morocco and Tunisia. In Morocco there is even a proposal to institute these
programs on a more permanent basis, given the frequency of climatic
shocks that adversely affect farmers there. In the Republic of Yemen the
limited labor content of public works programs has curtailed their role in
mitigating the problem of uninsured risk and transient poverty facing the
poor (van de Walle 2002).

Very few countries attempt to rigorously evaluate the targeting performance and poverty impact of public works programs. Van de Walle
(2004) has provided an assessment of targeting performance of a number
of poverty-related programs in Morocco, by comparing the geographic
distribution of spending against key poverty correlates at the provincial
level. The divergence between these two criteria permit some inference
of the underlying differences in mean benefits going to the poor rather
than the nonpoor, known as the *targeting differential*. A targeting differential that is positive indicates pro-poor targeting of program
expenditures.

Table 5.4 shows the degree of pro-poor targeting across several programs in Morocco, including some programs at different points in time.
For *Promotion Nationale* (PN) the evidence suggests that the program
benefited the nonpoor rather than the poor, with the amounts going to
the poor in both years not statistically different from zero. Nonetheless,
it is possible that spending within nonpoor provinces is reaching the
poorest groups because the design features of PN suggest a greater pos-
sibility for the poor to self-select into the program. Targeting under the
Barnamaj Al Aoulaouiyat Al Ijtimaiya (BAJ), including the PN component, is exceedingly pro-poor. Budget allocation under the program is
positively associated with poverty, particularly rural poverty. Specifically,
program allocations display a significant negative correlation with urban
poverty, which suggests that they are distributed to provinces with high
rural but low urban poverty. Targeting performance under the BAJ is enhanced where income differentiation is greater. Another successful program of transferring benefits to the poor is the Drought Prevention pro-

TABLE 5.4

Program Performance in Targeting the Poor in Morocco

(Moroccan Dirhams per capita)

Program	Actual Mean Per Capita Allocation	Estimated Mean Amount Going to Poor	Estimated Mean Amount Going to Nonpoor	Estimated Targeting Differential
Promotion Nationale 1994	104.0	0	124.6	−124.6
Promotion Nationale 2002	87.7	0	104.8	−104.8
BAJ1: PN component 1996–2003	20.2	122.7	0	122.7
BAJ1: Education and PN components 1997–2002	17.8	108.1	0	108.1
Drought Prevention 2001	119.5	353.9	67.4	286.4
		(3.3)	(3.2)	(2.2)
Drought Prevention 2002	121.4	334.1	74.9	259.2
		(2.4)	(2.7)	(1.6)
Entraide Nationale	1.2	4.6	0.6	4.0
		(2.8)	(2.1)	(2.1)

Source: van de Walle 2004, table 5.

Note: Barnamaj Al Aoulaouiyat Al Ijtimaiya (BAJ); PN Promotion Nationale. Numbers in parentheses are t-ratios. The targeting differential is the difference between the per capita spending amounts going to the poor and the amount going to the nonpoor. When an amount is negative, it is set to zero when calculating the targeting differential. All Moroccan Dirham amounts expressed in 2002 prices.

gram, which provides public works employment and pasture and herd protection. Although both the poor and nonpoor benefit from the program, the amounts received by the poor are estimated to be five times higher than those received by the nonpoor. Finally, despite a relatively small benefit amount, spending under *Entraide Nationale* is also pro-poor. The large variation in pro-poor impact across programs suggests that not all public works programs are created alike— differences in design make a huge difference in impact. Taking a more systematic approach to program evaluation, and collecting the detailed data necessary for this, should be considered a matter of high priority in Middle Eastern and North African countries.

Microfinance Programs

The microfinance industry in Middle Eastern and North African countries experienced significant growth over the last decade, with the number of active borrowers rising more than fivefold, from 129,000 active borrowers with an outstanding loan portfolio of $40 million to more than 710,000 with a loan portfolio of $240 million.[7] Until 2001 Egypt was the leader in the industry, but has since been overtaken by Morocco, which boasted more than 297,000 active borrowers in 2003, representing 42 percent of the region's active clients.

Coverage

Table 5.5 shows that there are approximately 0.7 million active clients of microfinance schemes in eight Middle Eastern and North African countries. This amounts to an estimated 19 percent of the potential client base. The size of the potential client base is estimated by assuming that 40 percent of all poor households would be eligible for a loan, and that poor households are those that live at or below 120 percent of the national poverty line for a given country. This yields a potential client pool of approximately 3.7 million households, or roughly five times the number of active borrowers. Thus about 3 million poor entrepreneur households still lack access to finance. Although this shows that a lot more needs to be done in this area, we also should acknowledge the rapid growth of the microfinance sector since the late-1990s when coverage was barely 3 percent.

Two other aspects of coverage may be noted. First, the region's microfinance industry has significantly improved its outreach to women, who now constitute 60 percent of all active clients, compared with only 36 percent in 1997. Jordan, Morocco, and the Republic of Yemen are the best performers in this regard. Second, the region's microfinance programs continue to be heavily urban oriented, with the proportion of rural clients typically being less than 25 percent and as low as 6 percent in the case of the Republic of Yemen. Only in Tunisia is there a substantial preference for rural clients who account for 57 percent of the total number of active borrowers there.

Sustainability

An increasing number of the region's microfinance institutions now adhere to good-practice financial standards with sustainability as an explicit objective. Indeed, such institutions are estimated to serve almost 90 percent of all active borrowers in their respective countries. A recent survey (see Brandsma and Burjorjee 2004) of 68 microfinance institutions in the region listed 17 programs (25 percent) as being fully financially sustainable in 2003. Of these, 7 were in Egypt serving 82 percent of the local market, and 5 were in Morocco serving 94 percent of the local market.

Even microfinance components in social fund programs are increasingly focusing on financial sustainability. First-generation social funds—those set up in the early 1990s—often placed a lot of emphasis on providing loans at subsidized rates. In contrast, newer social funds—those set up after 1995—tend to focus less on reaching disbursement targets and more on ensuring financial sustainability. In the Yemen Social Fund for Development, a case in point, the challenge in the first phase was to establish microfinance institutions where virtually none existed, and the objective in the second phase has

TABLE 5.5

Summary Statistics of Microfinance Indicators, 2003

Country	Active Borrowers (number)	Estimated Market Penetration[a]	Female Clients (%)	Rural Clients (%)	Fully Sustainable MFIs (number)	All MFIs and other Credit Programs in 2003 Sample (number)
Arab Republic of Egypt	256,159	16	46	13	7	20
Jordan	24,348	26	77	24	3	5
Lebanon	13,429	18	35	22	1	6
Morocco	297,148	45	75	23	5	7
Syria	32,170	8	—	—	0	6
Tunisia	63,736	41	46	57	1	2
West Bank/Gaza	13,394	10	41	31	0	7
Republic of Yemen	9,872	2	83	6	0	15
Total	710,256	19	60	22	17	68

Source: Adapted from Brandsma and Burjorjee 2004, p. 17, table 3.1.

Note: — Not available; MFI microfinance institution.

a. Market penetration equals the ratio of active borrowers to potential borrowers. The number of potential borrowers is calculated as 40 percent of all households spending less than 1.2 times the national poverty line in each country.

been to design lending terms and build institutional capability to provide services on a sustainable basis (Gross and de Silva 2002).

Notes

1. This report does not cover public pensions or public housing, although these may be considered part of the region's social protection arrangements. Pension systems in the Middle East and North Africa are the subject of a recent World Bank report (Robalino 2005).
2. This section draws on World Bank (1999a).
3. The Republic of Yemen example may be affected by pro-urban sampling biases in the 1992 survey. See World Bank (2002f).
4. The status of reforms in different countries and options for subsidy reform based on international experience are more fully analyzed in World Bank (1999a).
5. Needless to say, the pace and content of subsidy reforms also have been affected by political considerations. Initial attempts to modify food subsidies were met by public unrest in Egypt (1977), Jordan (1989), Morocco (1981), and Tunisia (1983). This underlines the sensitivity of the reforms and the need to mount a preemptive communications effort.
6. Subbarao (2003) also includes the mode of wage payment as a design feature because the form of payment, whether in cash or kind, could influence the participation of certain groups over others. This was the case in Lesotho and Zambia, for instance, where wage payment in the form of food elicited the participation of more women than men.
7. This section draws on Brandsma and Burjorjee (2004).

CHAPTER 6

Sustaining the Gains in Poverty Reduction and Human Development

Growth Strategy and Poverty Reduction

To recapitulate, since the mid-1980s the incidence of poverty in the Middle East and North Africa Region has fluctuated between 20 percent and 25 percent of the population (measured at the $2 line). Although it is low relative to that of other developing regions, the level of poverty in the Middle East and North Africa is substantial. On average, one of every four or five people in this region is poor. Moreover, vulnerability to poverty is quite high. Raising the level of the poverty line from $2 to $3 results in a near-doubling of the number of people who are poor from around 52 million to approximately 95 million (see table 1.5). This shows that a large number of people live so close to the poverty line that they can easily drop below it as a result of economic shocks. Therefore, the reduction of poverty should continue to be a major policy objective.

Stagnation in the rate of poverty reduction since the mid-1980s has accompanied stagnation in the rate of growth in per capita output (at around 1 percent annually) and shows that the region is not an exception to the general finding from within- and cross-country data that growth and poverty are strongly linked. Clearly the region's slow growth has exacted a social cost in the form of a lack of progress on the poverty front. Getting onto a higher growth trajectory will be critical to reducing the number and proportion of poor people in the region in the future. It also will be critical to reducing the number of unemployed people from its current level of around 13.4 percent—a level that surely could increase under the demographic pressures that the region now faces.

How is higher growth to be achieved? In a series of recent publications, the World Bank has presented a comprehensive analysis of the growth challenge for the region (World Bank 2004c, h, i). According to this analysis, to achieve higher growth on a sustainable basis, economies in the Middle East and North Africa must complete three fundamental realignments: (a) from public to private sector dominance, (b) from relatively closed to more open to international trade and investment, and (c) from excessive reliance on oil to more diversification.[1] Most countries in the region are already embarked on these realignments but more vigorous steps need to be to taken in the future to complete the transition. In addition, countries in the region need to pay greater attention to issues of governance because each transition implies deep changes in the role of government and improvements in its performance. The World Bank has calculated that an acceleration of the three realignments combined with measures to improve governance and increase the rate of female labor force participation will increase average output per capita by 3 percent annually or three times the actual rate experienced since the mid-1980s.

The quantitative importance of such a growth strategy to poverty reduction is illustrated in table 6.1. This table shows how poverty rates would move under two different growth scenarios: a 1 percent per capita annual growth path similar to that experienced during the last decade or so, and a 3 percent per capita annual path that is achievable under the strategy described above. Assuming no changes in the distribution of income, it is clear that the alternative growth paths imply very different poverty paths with significantly different outcomes within 10 to 12 years. For example, such a difference in growth will mean a 15 percentage point difference in poverty in the Republic of Yemen (29.2 percent versus 44.3 percent) by 2015 and in Egypt (10.4 percent versus 25.4 percent). For the region as a whole, the anticipated difference in poverty by 2015 is about 8 percentage points. Translated into numbers, this implies that the higher growth rate should lift an additional 22 million people out of poverty.

Although the growth strategy described above remains the most promising way to deal with the poverty and unemployment challenge faced by the region, it is useful to consider also the vulnerabilities that may be generated in the process. For example, whereas increased openness to trade and investment is likely to propel the region's economies onto a higher growth path, it also may create some adjustment challenges for certain groups in the short run. At the conceptual level, the link between openness and poverty is ambiguous.[2] On one hand, there are good reasons to expect the position of many poor groups to improve through the expansion of labor-intensive export sectors following trade liberalization. This has been the experience, for example, in many parts of East Asia where export-led economic growth has occurred. On the other hand, it is possible that the position of some groups among the poor could deteriorate. For example, some of those who lose jobs in the import-substituting sectors may be members of the poor population or may slide into poverty as a result.[3] Similarly, the price changes that accompany trade liberalization may have an adverse impact on some self-employed

TABLE 6.1

Poverty Forecasts at Alternative Economic Growth Rates

(Percent poor at the $2 line)

Country	Poverty Incidence at 1% Growth Rate			Poverty Incidence at 3% Growth Rate		
	2005	2010	2015	2005	2010	2015
Algeria	12.9	11.1	9.5	11.4	7.0	3.6
Egypt	33.5	29.4	25.4	30.3	19.2	10.4
Islamic Republic of Iran	4.5	3.5	2.3	3.5	2.5	1.5
Jordan	7.7	6.4	5.2	6.6	4.5	2.5
Morocco	11.3	9.5	7.8	9.9	5.0	2.5
Tunisia	5.2	4.1	3.2	4.4	2.5	1.5
Republic of Yemen	51.2	47.4	44.3	48.3	38.3	29.2
MENA7	19.1	16.9	14.8	17.2	11.6	7.1
MENA7 (millions)	45.6	44.3	42.5	41.1	30.3	20.6

Source: Staff calculations.

Note: MENA7 includes Algeria, Egypt, the Islamic Republic of Iran, Jordan, Morocco, Tunisia, and the Republic of Yemen.

poor people who may be net producers of commodities whose import is liberalized. A recent study done for Morocco suggested that removing protections from cereal could worsen the economic situation of some poor farmers who happen to be net producers of wheat (Ravallion and Lokshin 2004), even though it would be poverty reducing and welfare improving for the country as a whole.

The impact of transitional job losses can be mitigated by steps to improve the employability of workers through more flexible labor market laws and procedures. The socialist orientation of many Middle Eastern and North African governments in the post-independence period saw the introduction of labor laws that were, on balance, more concerned with job security and minimum incomes for the employed than with the business needs of private sector employers and the employment needs of potential workers. Although more flexibility with respect to regulations governing hiring has been introduced in some countries in recent years, rigidities in dismissals and layoffs continue to affect the levels and type of employment offered by the private sector. Many countries continue to ban dismissal for business reasons or make it administratively difficult and expensive.[4] As a result, formal private sector employment is lower than it needs to be.

Steps also can be taken to improve the employability of women in the private sector. As noted earlier, female labor force participation in the region is lower than what may be expected on the basis of achieved levels of female education and fertility. This outcome arises from a combination of social and economic factors, including a range of gender-based regulations that restrict the flexibility of female employment. Modifying such regulations to suit the needs of a modern economy and allow women greater flexibility to play multiple roles as both homemakers and workers would help in generating greater private sector employment opportunities for them.[5] Furthermore, the adoption of a more market-determined system of production is likely to lead to an increase in the demand for female labor, in contrast to the capital- and male-intensive patterns favored under public sector regimes (often involving infrastructure, construction, and energy projects). In recent decades Morocco and Tunisia have experienced significant increases in female employment in the textiles and garment industries operated by the private sector.

Finally, private sector and market orientation may increase inequality relative to a situation where public sector control of the economy compresses income and wage differences. This may affect poverty through one or both of two channels. First, it is commonly observed that higher levels of inequality lower the poverty-reduction impact of a given level of growth. Second, inequalities of income and wealth tend to lead to political maneuvering by the better-off groups to design institutions and policies to preserve their relative advantage (see World Bank 2006). Is inequality likely to increase under the trade- and market-oriented growth strategy? Recent experience is ambiguous on this point. In China and countries of the Former Soviet Union, the reduction of state control over the economy has allowed wage and income differentials to expand, leading to rising inequality. The same has happened in some countries of Latin America, although the mechanism there has involved greater dispersal of wage differentials by education levels as a consequence of trade liberalization. On the other hand, most studies of long-term trends in growth and inequality fail to show any systematic correlation between the two. And the experience of the high-performing East Asian countries (other than China) since the 1970s certainly has not followed the Latin American trend. In part this may have been because of a sustained effort in the East Asian countries to increase the supply of education and skills at a pace equal to evolving demand. This is an area in which the Middle Eastern and North African countries have done well in the past but still must continue to improve in the future.

Challenges for Human Development

Earlier chapters have shown that the Middle East and North Africa Region has performed well with regard to improvements in education and health indicators, generally considered to be important aspects of the non-income dimensions of poverty. Not only have such indicators improved over the past four decades, but also they have done so at a rate faster than the rate in comparator countries. And during the 1990s these improvements were achieved despite fiscal stringency and lower per capita spending on social services, thus suggesting both a greater role for private spending and gains in the efficiency of public spending. Nevertheless, good historical performance may not ensure similar performance in the future. The education and health challenges of the future are likely to be different from those of the past and will require different responses.

Challenges in Education

Although the region has a strong record of improving the *quantity* of education provided, the challenge of the future will be more in the area of education *quality* and labor-market relevance. As Middle Eastern and North African economies move toward producing more for world markets, they will need to compete with other countries to secure market share and obtain larger flows of foreign investment. The higher the level of skills in their workforces, the better placed the countries will be to compete internationally.

Improving the quality of education in public schools is of importance for poverty reduction and equity as well. Low quality in public schools is a special problem for poor children because they rarely have alternative higher-quality options in the form of private schools or private tutoring. Moreover, receiving a low-quality education at the primary and secondary levels effectively prevents children from poor backgrounds from passing the competitive examinations typically required for entrance to tertiary institutions.

Similarly, as Middle Eastern and North African economies become more private sector oriented, their respective education systems will need to produce skills that are in demand in the private sector. To achieve this, more attention will need to be paid to enhancing the *relevance* of education curricula. In most countries of the region, curricula were designed originally with a view to preparing graduates for public sector employment. Practical skills that are highly valued in the private sector are less prominent in the curricula and there exist few mechanisms for allowing private sector requirements to influence the content and standards of national curricula. Given the prospective importance of the private sector in future growth strategies for the region, it is important that education systems and curricula (including technical and vocational education) be reformed so as to support the private sector in this task.

The appropriate response to the education challenge of the future will involve going beyond the "engineering" approaches of the past that relied primarily on changing the quantity and mix of inputs (such as new buildings and equipment for schools) in the hope that this would deliver the necessary outputs. This was fine as long as the output was thought of in quantitative terms as the number of children enrolled in school or the number of computers per classroom and so on. However, when the definition of output changes to one in which quality is the most important dimension, new approaches must be developed. The challenges of the future will require the use of incentive mechanisms to motivate service providers to improve their performance, and accountability mechanisms to equip service receivers (students or their parents) to better enforce agreed-on standards of service delivery.[6]

Challenges in Health

Although the region has performed well in improving the access of the average citizen to primary care facilities and public health interventions, more needs to be done in the future on two fronts: further improving access for the poor and coping with an emerging disease pattern that is linked to lifestyle choices and an aging population. As noted earlier, despite substantial progress in the past four decades, significant disparities continue to exist between rich people and poor people with regard to health outcomes such as child mortality and malnutrition. For the most part, the removal of these disparities will require adequate funding of public health budgets, a continued special focus on maternal and child health services, and special efforts to target regions and neighborhoods with a preponderance of poor residents (such as most rural areas and urban slums). In addition to direct health interventions, it will be important to continue to address issues such as the supply of safe water and sanitation to underserved groups as well as to provide nutrition and preventive health education.

Coping with the disease patterns emerging from the demographic and epidemiologic transition, however, will require the development of new approaches to health care financing. Because the treatment of the emerging noncommunicable disease patterns is likely to be individual oriented and technology intensive, it will be costlier. Accordingly, there will be more pressure on budgetary resources, pressure that may take away funds that presently address the public health needs of the poor. Among ways to relieve such pressure are developing insurance mechanisms to spread the financial cost of treatment across a diversified pool of contributors and establishing charges for the use of university or highly specialized hospital services for those who can afford to pay. Because the new disease patterns also are spreading among the poor, it will be important to develop a system that provides them with low-cost access to treatment services as well. Also of relevance would be the redesign of existing subsidies (for example, on pharmaceuticals in the Islamic Republic of Iran) so as to minimize leakage to the nonpoor populace. This point is taken up in the next section.

Strengthening Social Safety Nets

Although measures directed at increasing growth and enhancing the access of the poor to health and education must remain the two principal pillars of the region's poverty reduction strategy, attention also will have to be paid to the third pillar— social safety nets. These must be reformed with two objectives in mind: (a) increasing the efficiency with which limited resources are directed to the needs of the poor and the vulnerable; and (b) improving their ability to cope with adverse, though temporary, income shocks that may occur as the economies become more private sector, trade, and market oriented. Indeed, improved efficiency can release resources not only to help those who need safety net assistance but also to increase pro-poor spending in other areas, such as public health, improved water supply, and better rural infrastructure. Finally, higher efficiency in reaching the poor through targeted assistance will have a greater impact on poverty reduction for any given level of growth of the economy and volume of fiscal resources devoted to the task.

Targeting Assistance to the Poor

Countries in the Middle East and North Africa Region have an extensive system of publicly funded social safety nets in addition to private arrangements linked to the tradition of *zakat* and other charitable activities. With respect to poverty reduction, the dilemma of the region's public safety nets may be baldly stated: the parts of the safety net that are effective are not efficient, and the parts that are relatively efficient are not effective. For example, food and energy subsidies reach a large number of people and are effective in the sense that they also reach the poor. However, both food and energy subsidies are inefficient in that they involve substantial leakage of benefits to nonpoor people. The benefits of energy subsidies, in particular, are heavily tilted toward the nonpoor. For example, as much as 93 percent of gasoline subsidies in Egypt go to the richest quintile. And the fiscal outlays are huge: energy subsidies in Egypt cost approximately 8.4 percent of GDP (in 2005), and they are thought to be even higher in the Islamic Republic of Iran. At the same time, other safety net components, such as cash transfers, are relatively better targeted to the poor and the vulnerable, but they are funded at such low levels (typically less than 1 percent of GDP) that they are not very effective in improving the conditions of the poor. The challenge for the future is to redesign social safety nets to focus the bulk of the available resources on the poor and the vulnerable populations.

There is both a political and a technical dimension to improving targeting. The political dimension arises from the resistance to be expected from those who stand to lose if subsidies are cut. Past attempts to reform subsidies have encountered such resistance in several Middle Eastern and North African countries, usually from the urban middle classes who feel squeezed between rising prices and stagnant incomes. The response to such resistance has varied across countries and over time. On some occasions, targeting efforts were abandoned and the subsidies were partially or fully restored. On others, the need to circumvent resistance led to more sophisticated program design (included self-targeting methods) and to flexibility in the pace and scope of the reform effort.

The technical dimension involves developing a cost-effective targeting mechanism. Because individual means-testing is costly in administrative terms, alternative approaches must be considered, including the use of such characteristics as literacy status, size of household, and location, or through inducing self-targeting. As discussed in an earlier chapter, reforms in Egypt and Tunisia have improved the targeting of food subsidies partly by introducing innovations that make it more likely that only the truly poor will seek to avail themselves of the subsidies. As a consequence, overall outlays on food subsidies have been reduced without notably affecting benefits to the poor. Geographic targeting also can be a cost-effective way to cover certain poverty groups that are relatively homogeneous, such as groups in rural or remote areas.

In the Middle East and North Africa Region, however, the ability to develop cost-effective targeting mechanisms is hampered by considerations of data access, quality, and use.

In order to target, public agencies must have good information about the location and other characteristics of the poor. They can be helped in identifying the poor if they share available data with nongovernment agencies and academic researchers with a professional interest in the subject. However, such data sharing is not common in the region. In some countries, household and labor market survey data are considered confidential. In others, they may not be considered confidential but are still made available only on a discretionary basis. Because such data are directly relevant to poverty and employment analysis, wider and easier access would be beneficial in formulating antipoverty policies.

Poverty analysis also can be improved if the underlying data are of relevance to the issues at hand. For example, it is useful to be able to distinguish between those who are chronically poor and those who are only temporarily poor. Regular mechanisms of economic growth may be an adequate way to help the latter group, but other assistance strategies may need to be devised for the former group. Identifying the chronically poor and understanding poverty dynamics require panel data (that is, data on the same families over time), and survey authorities in the Middle East and North Africa (with the exception of the Islamic Republic of Iran) do not typically collect such data.

Finally, effective antipoverty programs require monitoring and evaluation mechanisms so that results may be tracked and program design changed in accordance with the lessons of experience. This, in turn, requires an "evaluation culture" to prevail within government agencies dealing with poverty. Such a culture presently is lacking in most of the countries in the region.

Promoting Better Risk-Coping Mechanisms

As discussed above, a market-oriented development strategy can increase the risk of income shocks for some groups, leading to the need to find new jobs and set up new lines of business. Social policy in the Middle East and North Africa Region must develop better mechanisms to cope with this situation. The following instruments are especially relevant: unemployment insurance, temporary employment programs, and microfinance programs.

Having an unemployment benefits program in place can help workers transition from one job to another. This region features few programs of this nature. Formal unemployment insurance schemes paid for by contributions from firms and workers are rare. Where they exist, as in Algeria, Egypt, and the Islamic Republic of Iran, there are concerns about financial sustainability, incentives, and equity. Reserves in the insurance pool often are not allocated with a sufficient concern for long-run financial sustainability (see World Bank 2002d, pp. 73–74). Benefit periods tend to be on the long side, thus discouraging job search; and costs to employers are often on the high side, thus discouraging hiring. These aspects will have to be studied carefully to design unemployment insurance schemes that achieve social policy objectives at an affordable social cost.[7]

As discussed in the previous chapter, public works programs are commonly used to provide temporary employment in several Middle Eastern and North African countries. However, they differ widely in terms of program design, funding levels, and outcomes. In some cases jobs created through such programs have amounted to a significant proportion of the labor force (for example, 2.3 percent in Algeria and 2.7 percent in Tunisia), but it is not easy to assess whether these jobs have been created in an efficient manner (that is, at low cost) or even in an effective manner (that is, covering many of the poor). International experience suggests that cost-effective public works programs normally have high wage shares in total costs, and well-targeted programs normally offer wages below the prevailing market rate for unskilled labor and focus on geographic regions where poverty is high. These characteristics should be more systematically incorporated in public works programs in the Middle East and North Africa.

Having access to finance also helps people respond to business shocks. Because commercial banks rarely lend to the poor and the near-poor, the relevant issue for them is access to microfinance. In this region, microfinance is limited in scope and reach: almost 3 million entrepreneurial poor and vulnerable people still lack access to even the small amounts of finance that could help them run a microenterprise. However, the concept is growing in popularity and reach. Market penetration, or the number of people reached in relation to the number of potential clients (defined as 40 percent of those at or below 1.2 times the poverty line), was recently estimated at 19 percent and growing. Governments have been progressively lifting policy impediments to the growth and spread of microfinance, recognizing its potential to become a more important aspect of future social policy in the region.

Notes

1. Our concern is with trend growth over the long term. In the short run, such exogenous factors as increases in the price of oil can bring about growth spurts, as has been the case in 2003–05.
2. For a recent conceptual and empirical treatment of the subject of trade liberalization and poverty, see Winters, McCulloch, and McKay (2004). They concluded the following: "In the long run and on average, trade liberalization is likely to be strongly poverty alleviating, and there is no convincing evidence that it will generally increase overall poverty or vulnerability. But there is evidence that the poor may be less well placed in the short run to protect themselves against adverse effects and take advantage of favorable opportunities" (p. 72).
3. This may be an especially important consideration in economies where state-owned enterprises are prominent and especially in import-substituting sectors. In some cases the social challenge is compounded if a large proportion of employees in such companies is women.
4. Opportunities and constraints with respect to labor market reforms are discussed in World Bank (2004c).
5. Specific restrictions on women's work and mobility in the Middle East and North Africa Region are discussed in World Bank (2004b).
6. The scope, content, and limitations of various incentive and accountability mechanisms are being reviewed in an ongoing World Bank study of education reform in the region.
7. International experience shows that no unemployment income support program dominates other options in terms of performance. All have pros and cons, with different effects on labor market incentives and degrees of income insurance.

Estimating Poverty Rates

The World Bank is the principal source of information on poverty estimates. Its preferred method for preparing such estimates involves the following two initial steps: first, obtain real (1993 prices) data from nominal, local currency household *survey* data on mean consumption; and second, convert these data into PPP terms using the 1993 *consumption* (rather than *income*) PPP exchange rates.[1] Given data on distribution of expenditures, there are at least four steps for obtaining basic poverty and inequality statistics for a country at a particular point in time: (a) establish the poverty line in real terms for the base year, (b) obtain distribution data from surveys, (c) count the number/fraction of people below the poverty line for each region, and (d) aggregate upward for the country by weighting for different regions.

The above steps are taken when household survey data are available. If such data are not available, the following steps are involved:

- When a survey has not been conducted in a particular year, the distribution is taken from the *last* survey year; that is, it is assumed that the distribution remains unchanged from the last survey year.

- To update survey means, *growth* rates from national accounts data are used; that is, the survey mean from the last household survey is employed, along with the growth observed in per capita consumption from national accounts to obtain the mean estimate in the "new" non-survey year.

In some cases, even when a survey has been conducted, its results may not always be published or shared with the World Bank at an adequate level of disaggregation. This raises another methodological challenge for poverty analysts. How is a distribution to be obtained when unit record data (at the household level) are not available? Income distribution data sets like those of Deininger-Squire (1996) or the World Institute for Development Economics Research only present quintile shares of consumption (or income). One approach in using quintile data is to assume that all the persons within that quintile (20 percent of the population) obtain the *average* expenditure of that quintile. For poverty calculations, or for calculations of aggregate inequality, this assumption can sometimes be quite inaccurate. A procedure is needed to convert quintile expenditure shares into a lower level of aggregation, such as shares (and therefore mean expenditure levels) for each percentile of the population. When such unit record data are not available, the World Bank uses a Lorenz curve approximation.

Notes

1. Because data on income are thought to be less reliable than those on consumption, most poverty estimates actually work off consumption distributions. As long as income and consumption are related in a stable fashion over time, this should not affect assessments of the direction and scale of welfare changes.

GDP Per Capita (PPP) for the Middle East and North Africa Region and Comparator Countries, Selected Years, 1960–2000

	1960	1970	1980	1990	2000
Comparator country					
Angola	—	—	2,328	2,010	3,094
Bolivia	1,458	2,110	2,417	1,985	2,129
Brazil	2,759	3,764	6,667	6,046	6,695
Cameroon	1,974	1,970	2,352	1,871	1,584
Chile	3,384	4,229	4,516	5,415	8,268
Colombia	2,772	3,522	4,602	5,222	4,923
Costa Rica	3,640	5,043	6,359	5,750	7,595
Côte d'Ivoire	1,307	1,884	2,130	1,687	1,431
Dominican Republic	1,949	2,506	3,648	3,709	5,433
Ecuador	1,459	1,786	3,196	3,024	2,812
El Salvador	3,139	3,981	3,954	3,237	3,949
Ghana	1,825	2,162	1,752	1,487	1,724
Guatemala	2,447	2,989	3,735	3,070	3,355
Guinea	1,208	1,009	1,765	1,652	1,740
Haiti	1,709	1,395	1,564	1,322	9,79
Honduras	1,695	2,018	2,510	2,255	2,154
Indonesia	736	824	1,437	2,122	2,672
Jamaica	2,218	3,310	3,166	3,545	3,195
Republic of Korea	1,558	2,880	5,021	9,654	15,274
Malaysia	1,597	2,423	3,974	5,152	7962
Nicaragua	2,913	4,279	3,063	1,871	2,078
Papua New Guinea	1,503	2,308	2,021	1,718	2,002
Paraguay	2,396	2,838	4,673	4,263	3,886
Peru	3,262	4,420	5,092	3,535	4,214
Philippines	2,407	2,981	4,054	3,661	3,622
Sri Lanka	1,482	1,462	1,758	2,214	3,099
Thailand	1,061	1,718	2,436	4,170	5,621
Turkey	2,320	3,150	4,163	5,259	6,127
República Bolivariana de Venezuela	6,083	7,442	6,633	5,490	5,088
Zimbabwe	1,990	2,178	2,431	2,540	2,313
Middle East and North Africa					
Algeria	3,312	3,510	5,213	4,894	4,660
Arab Republic of Egypt	966	1,388	2,246	2,728	3,191
Islamic Republic of Iran	—	—	5,418	4,722	5,455
Jordan	1,353	1,655	4,211	3,592	3,482
Lebanon	4,529	5,521	6,696	2,033	3,783
Libya	2,809	3,572	4,317	3,800	3,625
Morocco	1,248	2,054	2,757	3,140	3,114
Syria	2,088	2,641	4,784	2,647	3,252
Tunisia	1,830	2,397	4,008	4,240	5,587
Republic of Yemen	773	856	1,392	1,944	859

Source: Staff calculations.

Note: — Not available.

Human Development Statistics: Selected Years

TABLE A.1

Population in the Middle East and North Africa, Selected Years, 1960–2004

(Millions)

Country	1960	1965	1970	1975	1980	1985	1990	1995	2000	2004
Algeria	10.8	11.9	13.7	16.0	18.7	21.9	25.0	28.1	30.4	32.4
Arab Republic of Egypt	25.9	29.4	33.1	36.3	40.9	46.5	52.4	58.2	64.0	68.7
Islamic Republic of Iran	21.6	24.7	28.4	33.2	39.1	47.1	54.4	59.0	63.7	66.9
Jordan	0.8	1.1	1.5	1.8	2.2	2.6	3.2	4.2	4.9	5.4
Lebanon	2.0	2.3	2.6	2.9	3.0	3.3	3.6	4.0	4.3	4.6
Libya	1.3	1.6	2.0	2.4	3.0	3.8	4.3	4.8	5.2	5.7
Morocco	11.6	13.3	15.3	17.3	19.4	21.6	24.0	26.4	28.7	30.6
Syria	4.6	5.3	6.3	7.4	8.7	10.4	12.1	14.2	16.2	17.8
Tunisia	4.2	4.6	5.1	5.6	6.4	7.3	8.2	9.0	9.6	10.0
Republic of Yemen	5.2	5.8	6.3	7.0	8.5	10.1	11.9	15.2	17.5	19.8

Source: World Development Indicators 2004.

Note: —Not available.

TABLE A.2

Life Expectancy at Birth, Total Population, Selected Years, 1960–2003

(Years)

Country	1960	1965	1970	1975	1980	1985	1990	1995	2000	2003
Algeria	47.3	50.2	53.3	56.3	59.3	63.6	67.4	69.5	70.5	70.9
Arab Republic of Egypt	46.4	48.8	51.1	53.3	55.5	59.3	62.8	65.3	67.8	69.1
Islamic Republic of Iran	47.8	50.2	52.8	55.5	58.1	61.5	64.7	67.1	68.8	69.4
Jordan	54.3	56.6	58.9	61.2	63.5	65.8	68.5	70.4	71.5	72.1
Lebanon	59.8	62.0	64.2	65.0	65.0	66.2	67.9	69.3	70.4	70.9
Libya	46.9	49.4	51.9	55.7	60.5	65.2	68.5	69.9	71.5	72.7
Morocco	46.9	49.4	51.9	54.6	58.0	61.0	63.5	65.7	67.7	68.6
Syria	50.0	52.8	55.8	58.8	61.6	64.0	66.4	68.3	69.7	70.5
Tunisia	48.6	51.1	54.2	58.6	62.4	65.2	70.3	71.4	72.1	73.2
Republic of Yemen	36.3	38.6	41.3	45.0	48.5	50.8	52.2	54.1	56.5	57.7

Source: World Development Indicators 2004.

Note: —Not available.

TABLE A.3

Life Expectancy at Birth, Female, Selected Years, 1960–2003
(Years)

Country	1960	1965	1970	1975	1980	1985	1990	1995	2000	2003
Algeria	48.4	51.3	54.3	57.3	60.3	64.8	68.8	70.9	71.9	72.3
Arab Republic of Egypt	47.6	50.0	52.4	54.5	56.8	60.5	64.3	67.0	69.5	70.8
Islamic Republic of Iran	47.7	50.0	52.5	55.6	59.4	62.7	65.4	67.9	69.7	70.5
Jordan	55.9	58.2	60.5	62.8	65.1	67.4	70.3	72.2	73.2	73.8
Lebanon	61.7	63.9	66.1	67.0	67.0	68.2	69.9	71.2	72.2	72.7
Libya	48.2	50.8	53.4	57.4	62.2	67.1	70.4	71.8	73.8	75.3
Morocco	48.2	50.8	53.4	56.3	59.8	62.8	65.3	67.6	69.6	70.7
Syria	51.3	54.3	57.4	60.6	63.4	65.9	68.5	70.6	72.1	72.9
Tunisia	49.1	51.6	54.7	59.3	63.5	66.4	72.1	73.3	74.2	75.3
Republic of Yemen	36.5	38.8	41.6	46.2	49.7	51.4	52.6	54.5	57.1	58.4

Source: World Development Indicators 2004.
Note: —Not available.

TABLE A.4

Mortality Rate for Children under 5 Years of Age, Selected Years, 1960–2003
(Per 1,000 live births)

Country	1960	1965	1970	1975	1980	1985	1990	1995	2000	2003
Algeria	280	257	234	184	134	102	69	55	45	41
Arab Republic of Egypt	278	257	235	204	173	139	104	71	49	39
Islamic Republic of Iran	281	236	191	161	130	101	72	55	44	39
Jordan	139	123	107	87	65	55	40	35	30	28
Lebanon	85	70	54	49	44	41	37	34	32	31
Libya	270	215	160	115	70	56	42	29	20	16
Morocco	211	198	184	164	144	115	85	61	46	39
Syria	201	165	129	101	74	59	44	31	22	18
Tunisia	254	228	201	151	100	76	52	37	28	24
Republic of Yemen	340	322	303	254	205	174	142	126	117	113

Source: World Development Indicators 2004.
Note: —Not available.

TABLE A.5

Adult Male and Female Literacy, Selected Years, 1970–2002

(Percentage of people age 15 years and older)

Country	1970	1975	1980	1985	1990	1995	2000	2002
Algeria	21.5	28.4	36.6	44.9	52.9	60.3	66.7	69.8
Arab Republic of Egypt	31.6	35.4	39.3	43.2	47.1	55.6	—	—
Islamic Republic of Iran	34.3	42.0	49.7	55.9	63.2	70.0	76.0	77.0
Jordan	55.1	62.3	69.2	75.6	81.5	86.5	89.8	89.9
Lebanon	—	—	—	—	—	—	—	—
Libya	35.4	44.7	52.7	60.8	68.1	74.5	79.9	81.7
Morocco	19.8	24.5	28.6	33.5	38.7	43.9	48.8	50.7
Syria	41.1	47.7	53.3	59.4	64.8	69.9	74.4	82.9
Tunisia	27.4	36.3	44.9	52.6	59.1	64.7	71.0	74.3
Republic of Yemen	14.2	14.9	20.0	25.9	32.7	40.1	46.4	49.0

Source: World Bank EdStats, www.worldbank.org/education/edstats.

Note: —Not available. Italic type indicates data taken from closest available year. The most recent literacy data for the Islamic Republic of Iran is from 2001.

TABLE A.6

Adult Female Literacy, Selected Years, 1970–2002

(Percentage of females age 15 years and older)

Country	1970	1975	1980	1985	1990	1995	2000	2002
Algeria	11.6	17.2	24.5	33.1	41.3	49.5	57.0	60.1
Arab Republic of Egypt	16.8	20.5	24.7	29.1	33.6	43.6	—	—
Islamic Republic of Iran	22.9	30.3	38.2	45.9	54.0	61.9	68.9	70.4
Jordan	36.8	45.7	55.4	64.4	72.1	79.4	84.3	84.7
Lebanon	—	—	—	—	—	—	—	—
Libya	12.2	20.6	30.5	41.0	51.1	60.2	68.1	70.7
Morocco	8.2	11.7	15.5	20.0	25.0	30.5	36.1	38.3
Syria	21.0	27.2	33.8	40.8	47.5	54.1	60.5	74.2
Tunisia	14.8	22.9	31.2	39.0	46.5	53.3	60.6	65.4
Republic of Yemen	2.3	3.6	5.5	8.5	12.9	18.5	25.3	28.5

Source: World Bank EdStats, www.worldbank.org/education/edstats.

Note: —Not available. Italic type indicates data taken from closest available year.

TABLE A.7

Average Years of Schooling, Total Population Age 15 Years and Older, Selected Years 1960–2000

Country	1960	1965	1970	1975	1980	1985	1990	1995	2000
Algeria	0.98	1.04	1.56	2.01	2.68	3.46	4.25	4.83	5.37
Arab Republic of Egypt	—	—	—	1.55	2.34	3.56	4.26	4.98	5.51
Islamic Republic of Iran	0.80	1.34	1.61	2.21	2.82	3.37	3.96	4.73	5.31
Jordan	2.33	2.74	3.25	3.77	4.28	5.23	5.95	6.47	6.91
Lebanon	—	—	—	—	—	—	—	—	—
Libya	—	0.97	—	2.03	—	3.87	—	—	—
Morocco	—	—	—	—	—	—	—	—	—
Syria	1.35	1.77	2.15	2.84	3.65	4.47	5.11	5.48	5.78
Tunisia	0.61	0.94	1.48	2.27	2.94	3.34	3.94	4.53	5.01
Republic of Yemen	—	—	—	0.09	0.34	0.84	1.49	—	—

Source: World Bank EdStats, www.worldbank.org/education/edstats.

Note: —Not available.

TABLE A.8

Average Years of Schooling, Females Age 15 Years and Older, Selected Years 1960–2000

Country	1960	1965	1970	1975	1980	1985	1990	1995	2000
Algeria	0.78	0.94	0.77	1.16	1.77	2.51	3.27	3.94	4.53
Arab Republic of Egypt	—	—	—	0.93	1.56	2.42	3.15	3.91	4.48
Islamic Republic of Iran	0.41	0.81	1.04	1.50	2.00	2.57	3.15	3.93	4.54
Jordan	1.21	1.57	2.07	2.45	3.26	4.40	5.24	5.68	6.05
Lebanon	—	—	—	—	—	—	—	—	—
Libya	—	0.18	—	0.73	—	2.79	—	—	—
Morocco	—	—	—	—	—	—	—	—	—
Syria	0.58	0.83	1.06	1.62	2.37	3.19	3.89	4.38	4.77
Tunisia	0.25	0.49	0.91	1.49	1.99	2.34	3.00	3.67	4.23
Republic of Yemen	—	—	—	0.01	0.07	0.17	0.48	—	—

Source: World Bank EdStats, www.worldbank.org/education/edstats.

Note: —Not available.

TABLE A.9

Public Expenditure on Education, Selected Years, 1970–2002
(Percent of GDP)

Country	1970	1975	1980	1985	1990	1995	2000	2002
Algeria	7.72	6.64	7.60	8.32	5.31	5.43	—	—
Arab Republic of Egypt	4.74	5.03	5.30	5.67	3.89	4.67	—	—
Islamic Republic of Iran	—	—	7.51	3.65	4.08	4.08	4.64	4.94
Jordan	3.81	3.83	6.79	6.79	8.06	8.23	4.95	—
Lebanon	—	—	—	—	3.24	2.73	2.04	2.68
Libya	3.94	5.95	3.38	7.09	—	—	2.67	—
Morocco	3.47	5.21	5.89	5.94	5.27	5.60	6.40	6.49
Syria	3.85	3.95	4.58	6.08	4.00	3.18	—	—
Tunisia	6.81	5.03	5.24	5.54	5.99	6.48	6.84	6.37
Republic of Yemen	—	—	—	—	—	4.49	9.89	9.55

Source: World Bank EdStats, www.worldbank.org/education/edstats.

Note: —Not available. Italic type indicates data taken from closest available year.

TABLE A.10

Gross Primary School Enrollment, Total Population, Selected Years, 1970–2002
(Percent of relevant age group)

Country	1970	1975	1980	1985	1990	1995	2000	2002
Algeria	76.1	92.7	94.5	93.6	100.5	106.6	107.4	108.7
Arab Republic of Egypt	67.6	70.0	73.1	85.4	91.5	99.8	96.6	97.4
Islamic Republic of Iran	72.8	93.2	87.3	98.2	109.3	101.0	93.0	91.9
Jordan	72.1	86.6	81.7	71.8	73.3	71.3	97.0	99.1
Lebanon	121.4	—	111.4	111.8	113.2	109.4	102.5	103.4
Libya	110.5	137.3	124.6	108.6	104.7	118.0	114.6	114.2
Morocco	51.5	62.0	83.0	77.2	65.2	83.8	101.2	109.6
Syria	77.5	95.6	99.6	109.6	102.2	100.8	108.6	114.9
Tunisia	100.4	96.5	102.1	115.1	113.7	116.8	112.9	110.7
Republic of Yemen	—	—	—	—	65.4	73.1	79.2	83.5

Source: World Bank EdStats, www.worldbank.org/education/edstats.

Note: —Not available. Italic type indicates data taken from closest available year.

TABLE A.11

Gross Female Primary School Enrollment, Selected Years, 1970–2002

(Percent of relevant age group)

Country	1970	1975	1980	1985	1990	1995	2000	2002
Algeria	58.2	75.5	80.7	83.5	92.0	100.4	102.9	104.5
Arab Republic of Egypt	52.8	55.8	61.0	76.2	82.8	93.1	93.1	94.7
Islamic Republic of Iran	52.1	71.4	—	87.1	103.4	97.6	90.9	90.4
Jordan	64.9	81.7	81.2	72.2	74.1	71.8	97.2	99.5
Lebanon	111.9	—	—	—	110.9	107.7	100.7	101.7
Libya	83.7	129.7	120.5	103.8	101.3	118.3	115.5	114.1
Morocco	36.1	45.2	62.9	60.2	52.9	71.6	94.1	103.7
Syria	58.9	78.3	87.7	102.3	96.6	95.5	104.7	111.6
Tunisia	79.5	77.3	86.8	105.2	106.8	112.6	110.4	108.6
Republic of Yemen	—	—	—	—	33.6	41.5	61.0	68.0

Source: World Bank EdStats, www.worldbank.org/education/edstats.

Note: —Not available. Italic type indicates data taken from closest available year.

TABLE A.12

Gross Secondary School Enrollment, Total Population, Selected Years 1970–2002

(Percent of relevant age group)

Country	1970	1975	1980	1985	1990	1995	2000	2002
Algeria	11.2	20.0	33.0	51.4	60.9	62.5	77.7	80.0
Arab Republic of Egypt	28.4	40.3	50.5	61.4	70.8	76.5	85.3	85.3
Islamic Republic of Iran	27.1	45.0	41.9	45.0	57.5	75.0	77.3	77.9
Jordan	32.8	47.5	59.1	52.2	63.3	55.3	86.1	86.0
Lebanon	41.5	46.9	59.1	60.6	73.9	80.6	75.5	79.4
Libya	20.8	54.7	75.9	58.8	95.2	101.5	104.8	104.7
Morocco	12.6	16.5	26.0	35.4	35.5	38.5	40.9	45.0
Syria	38.1	43.0	46.4	58.2	48.8	43.3	42.8	48.4
Tunisia	22.7	21.1	27.0	38.9	44.4	60.4	77.6	77.6
Republic of Yemen	—	—	—	—	45.4	30.6	46.3	47.3

Source: World Bank EdStats, www.worldbank.org/education/edstats.

Note: —Not available. Italic type indicates data taken from closest available year.

TABLE A.13

Gross Female Secondary School Enrollment, Selected Years, 1970–2002

(Percent of relevant age group)

Country	1970	1975	1980	1985	1990	1995	2000	2002
Algeria	6.5	13.7	25.9	43.6	54.2	59.1	*79.6*	82.7
Arab Republic of Egypt	18.7	28.6	38.8	50.4	62.4	70.5	82.4	82.4
Islamic Republic of Iran	18.1	32.5	31.8	35.8	49.0	68.7	75.0	75.4
Jordan	23.4	39.8	56.1	54.3	64.8	57.4	*87.3*	86.9
Lebanon	33.5	46.5	57.0	60.0	*76.3*	84.3	79.3	82.8
Libya	7.8	37.8	62.6	56.8	*95.6*	98.1	*108.0*	108.0
Morocco	7.4	11.8	19.7	28.3	29.9	32.9	36.5	40.8
Syria	20.8	28.1	35.1	47.5	41.1	40.1	40.4	46.2
Tunisia	12.6	14.6	20.2	31.8	39.0	79.7	79.7	80.7
Republic of Yemen	—	—	—	—	*15.5*	12.8	26.9	29.2

Source: World Bank EdStats, www.worldbank.org/education/edstats.

Note: —Not available. Italic type indicates data taken from closest available year.

Millennium Development Goals and Performance

TABLE A.14

Goal 1: Eradicate Extreme Poverty and Hunger

Country	Prevalence of underweight in children under five years of age			Share of population below minimum level of dietary energy consumption (%)	
	1990	2000	2003	1997	2001
Algeria	9.2	6.0	—	6.0	5.0
Arab Republic of Egypt	10.4	4.0	8.6	3.0	4.0
Islamic Republic of Iran	*15.7*	*10.9*	—	3.0	4.0
Jordan	6.4	*5.1*	*4.4*	7.0	8.0
Lebanon	—	3.0	—	3.0	3.0
Libya	—	*4.7*	—	2.5	2.5
Morocco	9.5	*9.0*	—	6.0	7.0
Syria	*12.1*	6.9	—	4.0	4.0
Tunisia	*10.3*	4.0	—	2.5	2.5
Republic of Yemen	*30.0*	*46.1*	—	36.0	36.0

Source: World Development Indicators 2004.

Note: —Not available. Italic type indicates data taken from closest available year.

TABLE A.15

Goal 2: Achieve Universal Primary Education

Country	Net primary enrollment rate (% of relevant age group)			Primary completion rate, total (% of relevant age group)		
	1990	2000	2002	1990	2000	2003
Algeria	93.2	94.2	94.9	80.4	95.5	*95.5*
Arab Republic of Egypt	83.7	89.9	91.4	—	99.6	90.8
Islamic Republic of Iran	92.3	79.2	86.3	100.5	104.6	*107.3*
Jordan	94.1	*91.3*	92.0	103.6	*102.7*	*98.2*
Lebanon	77.8	89.7	90.6	—	71.1	67.9
Libya	96.1	—	—	—	—	—
Morocco	56.8	83.7	89.6	47.2	61.1	75.0
Syria	92.3	95.9	97.9	98.6	86.5	*87.5*
Tunisia	93.9	95.4	97.3	74.5	91.1	101.2
Republic of Yemen	51.7	67.1	71.8	—	57.9	65.5

Source: World Development Indicators 2004.

Note: —Not available. Italic type indicates data taken from closest available year.

TABLE A.16

Goal 3: Promote Gender Equality and Empower Women

Country	Ratio of girls to boys in primary and secondary education (%)			Ratio of young literate females to males, ages 15–24 (%)		
	1990	2000	2002	1990	2000	2002
Algeria	83.3	*97.7*	98.6	79.1	89.6	91.1
Arab Republic of Egypt	81.3	93.4	94.2	72.0	*84.7*	—
Islamic Republic of Iran	84.5	94.9	95.2	88.1	94.9	95.6
Jordan	101.4	*101.1*	101.3	97.3	100.2	100.3
Lebanon	—	102.0	101.9	92.8	95.7	96.1
Libya	—	*103.2*	103.2	83.5	93.2	94.2
Morocco	70.1	85.1	87.8	61.8	76.5	79.2
Syria	84.8	92.0	93.5	72.5	82.6	84.2
Tunisia	85.6	100.0	101.7	81.0	91.5	82.5
Republic of Yemen	—	55.6	60.8	34.1	55.7	60.3

Source: World Development Indicators 2004.

Note: —Not available. Italic type indicates data taken from closest available year.

TABLE A.17

Goal 4: Reduce Child Mortality

Country	Infant mortality rate (per 1,000 live births)			Under 5 mortality rate (per 1,000 children)		
	1990	2000	2002	1990	2000	2003
Algeria	54	37	35	69	45	41
Arab Republic of Egypt	76	40	33	104	49	39
Islamic Republic of Iran	54	36	33	72	44	39
Jordan	33	25	23	40	30	28
Lebanon	32	28	27	37	32	31
Libya	34	17	13	42	20	16
Morocco	66	41	36	85	46	39
Syria	35	19	16	44	22	18
Tunisia	41	22	19	52	28	24
Republic of Yemen	98	84	82	142	117	113

Source: World Development Indicators 2004.

TABLE A.18

Goal 5: Improve Maternal Health

Country	Maternal mortality ratio per 100,000 live births			Births attended by skilled health professional (%)
	1990	1995	2000	Most recent
Algeria	160	150	140	92
Arab Republic of Egypt	*170*	*170*	*84*	69
Islamic Republic of Iran	*120*	*130*	*76*	90
Jordan	150	*41*	*41*	100
Lebanon	300	130	150	89
Libya	220	120	97	94
Morocco	*610*	*390*	*220*	40
Syrian Arab Republic	*180*	200	160	76
Tunisia	170	70	120	90
Republic of Yemen	1,400	*850*	*570*	22

Source: UN Statistics Division and World Development Indicators, 2004.

Note: Maternal mortality ratios are modeled estimates, except those in italics which are from country survey or registration data. Attended births data range from 1995-2000.

TABLE A.19

Goal 6: Combat HIV/AIDS, Malaria, and Tuberculosis

Country	Contraceptive prevalence rate of women, ages 15–49			Incidence of tuberculosis (per 100,000 people)		
	1990	2000	2002	1990	2000	2003
Algeria	*50.8*	—	57.0	36.4	48.4	52.8
Arab Republic of Egypt	*47.6*	56.1	60.0	41.8	30.8	28.1
Islamic Republic of Iran	*49.0*	74.0	—	40.9	30.7	28.2
Jordan	35.0	*50.3*	56.0	12.5	6.1	4.9
Lebanon	—	63.0	—	42.7	16.4	12.3
Libya	—	*45.0*	—	31.0	22.8	20.8
Morocco	*41.5*	59.0	—	134.2	117.0	112.3
Syria	*40.0*	*45.3*	48.0	68.2	47.3	42.4
Tunisia	*49.8*	66.0	—	38.0	25.0	22.1
Republic of Yemen	9.7	*20.8*	23.0	137.6	101.4	92.5

Source: World Development Indicators 2004.

Note: —Not available. Italic type indicates data taken from closest available year.

TABLE A.20

Goal 7: Ensure Environmental Sustainability

Country	Access to improved water source (% of population)		Access to improved sanitation (% of population)		CO2 emissions (metric tons per capita)	
	1990	2002	1990	2002	1990	2002
Algeria	95	87	88	92	3.2	2.9
Arab Republic of Egypt	94	98	54	68	1.4	2.2
Islamic Republic of Iran	91	93	83	84	3.9	4.9
Jordan	98	91	—	93	3.2	3.2
Lebanon	100	100	—	98	2.5	3.5
Libya	71	72	97	97	8.8	10.9
Morocco	75	80	57	61	1.0	1.3
Syria	79	79	76	77	3.0	3.3
Tunisia	77	82	75	80	1.6	1.9
Republic of Yemen	69	69	21	30	*0.7*	0.5

Source: World Development Indicators 2004.

Note: —Not available. Italic type indicates data taken from closest available year.

TABLE A.21

Goal 8: Develop a Global Partnership for Development

Country	Personal computers per 100 population			Internet users per 100 population		
	1995	2000	2003	1995	2000	2003
Algeria	0.30	0.66	0.83	0.00	0.49	1.60
Arab Republic of Egypt	0.43	1.26	2.91	0.03	0.71	4.37
Islamic Republic of Iran	2.53	6.28	9.05	0.00	0.98	7.24
Jordan	0.82	2.98	4.47	0.02	2.45	8.11
Lebanon	1.66	5.32	10.00	0.08	9.13	14.29
Libya	—	—	2.34	—	0.18	2.89
Morocco	0.32	1.22	1.99	0.00	0.70	3.32
Syrian Arab Republic	0.71	1.54	*1.94*	0.00	0.19	*1.29*
Tunisia	0.67	2.29	4.05	0.01	2.72	6.37
Republic of Yemen	*0.09*	0.19	*0.74*	0.00	0.08	*0.51*

Source: World Development Indicators, 2004

Note: —Not available. Computer data in italics are from the closest available year.

Bibliography

Adams, Richard H. 1991. "The Economic Uses and Impact of International Remittances in Rural Egypt." *Economic Development and Cultural Change* 39 (4): 695–722.

Adams, Richard H. 2000. "Self-Targeted Subsidies: The Distributional Impact of the Egyptian Food Subsidy System." Policy Research Working Paper 2322, World Bank, Washington, DC.

Adams, Richard H., and John Page. 2003. "Poverty, Inequality and Growth in Selected Middle East and North Africa Countries, 1980–2000." *World Development* 31 (12): 2027–48.

Alderman, Harold, and Kathy Lindert. 1998. "The Potential and Limitations of Self-Targeted Food Subsidies." *World Bank Research Observer* 13 (2): 213–29.

Assaad, Ragui, and Malak Rouchdy. 1999. "Poverty and Poverty Alleviation Strategies in Egypt." Cairo Papers in Social Science, 22:1, American University of Cairo.

Bhalla, Surjit. 2002. *Imagine There's No Country. Poverty, Inequality and Growth in the Era of Globalization.* Washington, DC: Institute for International Economics.

Brandsma, Judith, and Deena Burjorjee. 2004. "Microfinance in the Arab States: Building Inclusive Financial Sectors." New York: United Nations Capital Development Fund.

Carnoy, Martin. 2005. "Education, Economic Growth, and the Distribution of Economic Benefits in the MENA Region: Lessons from the Past Thirty Years." Background paper for World Bank Education Report for MENA Region (forthcoming).

Deininger, Klaus, and Lyn Squire. 1996. *A New Database on International Income Distribution.* Washington, DC: World Bank.

El-Laithy, H., and K. Abu-Ismail. 2005. *Poverty in Syria: 1996–2004.* New York: United Nations Development Programme.

Gross, Alexandra, and Samantha de Silva. 2002. "Social Fund Support of Microfinance: A Review of Implementation Experience." Social Protection Discussion Paper 0215, World Bank, Washington, DC.

Iqbal, Farrukh, and Nagwa Riad. 2004. "Increasing Girls' School Enrolment in the Arab Republic of Egypt." Mimeographed. World Bank. Washington, DC.

Mehryar, Amir. 2004. "Primary Health Care and the Rural Poor in the Islamic Republic of Iran." Mimeographed. World Bank, Washington, DC.

Psacharopoulos, George, and Harry Anthony Patrinos. 2002. "Returns to Investment in Education: A Further Update." Policy Research Working Paper 2881, World Bank, Washington, DC.

Ravallion, Martin, and Michael Lokshin. 2004. "Gainers and Losers from Trade Reform in Morocco." Working Paper 37, Middle East and North Africa Region, World Bank, Washington, DC.

Robalino, David. 2005. *Pensions in the Middle East and North Africa: Time for Change*. Washington, DC: World Bank.

Royaume du Maroc, Haut Commissariat au Plan. 2005. *Enquete Nationale Sur La Consommation et les Depenses Des Menages 2000/01*. Rabat, Morocco.

Shaban, Radwan, Dina Abu-Ghaida, and A. S. Al-Naimat. 2001. *Poverty Alleviation in Jordan: Lessons for the Future*. Washington, DC: World Bank.

Subbarao, Kalanidhi. 2003. "Systemic Shocks and Social Protection: Role and Effectiveness of Public Works Programs." Social Protection Discussion Paper 0302, World Bank, Washington, DC.

UNDP (United Nations Development Programme). 2002. *Arab Human Development Report 2002: Creating Opportunities for Future Generations*. New York: United Nations.

van de Walle, Dominique. 2004. "Do Basic Services and Poverty Programs Reach Morocco's Poor? Evidence from Poverty and Spending Maps." Working Paper 41, Middle East and North Africa Region, World Bank, Washington, DC.

van de Walle, Dominique. 2002. "Poverty and Transfers in Yemen." Working Paper 30, Middle East and North Africa Region, World Bank, Washington, DC.

WBI (World Bank Institute). 2004. "Public Health in the Middle East and North Africa: Meeting the Challenges of the Twenty-First Century." Learning Resource Series Publication 29163, Washington, DC.

Winters, Alan, Neil McCulloch, and Andrew McKay. 2004. "Trade Liberalization and Poverty: The Evidence So Far." *Journal of Economic Literature* 42 (1): 72–115.

World Bank. 2006. *World Development Report: Equity and Development*. Washington, DC.

———. 2005a. *Rebuilding Iraq: Economic Reform and Transition*. Washington, DC.

———. 2005b. "Egypt: Toward a More Effective Social Policy: Subsidies and Social Safety Net." Report 33550-EG, Washington, DC.

———. 2004a. *Algerie: La Pauvrete En 2000 En Algerie*. Washington, DC.

———. 2004b. "Arab Republic of Egypt: A Poverty Reduction Strategy for Egypt." Report 27954-EGT, Washington, DC.

———. 2004c. *Gender and Development in the Middle East and North Africa: Women in the Public Sphere*. Washington, DC.

———. 2004d. "The Hashemite Kingdom of Jordan: Poverty Assessment." Report 27658-JO, Washington, DC.

———. 2004e. "Kingdom of Morocco Poverty Report: Strengthening Policy by Identifying the Geographic Dimension of Poverty." Report 28223-MOR, Washington, DC.

———.2004f. *Policy Note on Budgetary and Poverty Impacts of Petroleum Pricing in Yemen*. Washington, DC.

———. 2004g. *Poverty in the West Bank and Gaza after Three Years of Economic Crisis*. Washington, DC.

———. 2004h. *Trade, Investment and Development in the Middle East and North Africa: Engaging with the World*. Washington, DC.

———. 2004i. *Unlocking the Employment Potential in the Middle East and North Africa: Toward a New Social Contract*. Washington, DC.

———. 2003a. "Poverty in Iran: Trends and Structure, 1986–1998." Report 24414-IR, Washington, DC.

———. 2003b. "Republic of Tunisia: Poverty Update." MENA Region Social and Economic Development Group, Washington, DC.

———. 2002a. "Arab Republic of Egypt: Poverty Reduction in Egypt, Diagnosis and Strategy." Report. 24234-EGT. Washington, DC.

———. 2002b. "Kingdom of Morocco: Social Protection Note." MENA Region Human Development Group, Washington, DC.

———. 2002c. "Public Health in the Middle East and North Africa: A Situation Analysis." Human Development Network, Washington, DC.

———. 2002d. *Reducing Vulnerability and Increasing Opportunity: Social Protection in the Middle East and North Africa*. Washington, DC.

———. 2002e. "Republic of Yemen: Poverty Update." Report 24422-YEM, Washington, DC.

———. 2001. "Kingdom of Morocco: Poverty Update." Report 21506-MOR, Washington, DC.

———. 2000. *Making Transition Work for Everyone: Poverty and Inequality in Europe and Central Asia*. Washington, DC.

———. 1999a. "Consumer Food Subsidy Programs in the MENA Region." Report 19561-MNA, Washington, DC.

———. 1999b. "Democratic and Popular Republic of Algeria: Growth, Employment and Poverty Reduction." Report 18564-AL, Washington, DC.

———. 1996. "Republic of Tunisia: From Universal Food Subsidies to a Self-Targeted Program." Report 15878-TUN, Washington, DC.

Index